AF344401

12 CLASSIC ARCH BOOKS

CONCORDIA PUBLISHING HOUSE • SAINT LOUIS

Arch® Books

Published 2022 by Concordia Publishing House

3558 S. Jefferson Ave., St. Louis, MO 63118-3968

1-800-325-3040 • cph.org

Arch Books TREASURY

Christmas Collection

Table of Contents

Dear Parents,

For God so loved the world, that He gave His only Son, that whoever believes in Him should not perish but have eternal life.

John 3:16

Parents and educators are given the wonderful responsibility of teaching children about God and His will for them. One of the ways we do this is by teaching them God's Word—the Bible. Since the first Arch Books were published in the mid-1960s, the series has existed for the sole purpose of teaching the Bible to children. More than 400 different Arch Books have been published. And through them, millions of children have learned about biblical people and events, about faith and forgiveness, and about the Gospel of Jesus Christ.

Now, as this beloved series enters its sixth decade, Concordia Publishing House is rereleasing this collection of Arch Books to commemorate the series's legacy and to celebrate its influence on Bible literacy. This collection reproduces the original words and pictures.

To God be the glory!

The Editor

QUALITY RELIGIOUS BOOKS FOR CHILDREN
ARCH BOOKS
Mary's Story
193

Mary's Story

LUKE 1:5 – 2:18 FOR CHILDREN

Written by M. M. Brem
Illustrated by Sally Mathews

Concordia Publishing House

One day as Mary washed her clothes,
she had a sudden scare.
And how she jumped! She was surprised
to see an angel there.

Before she had a chance to speak,
the angel said, "Don't fear.
I have important news for you.
Our God has sent me here.

"For you will have a baby soon,
and He will be God's Son.
His name is Jesus. He will come
in love for everyone."

"But I'm not married yet," she said.
"So how can this be true?"
"That isn't hard for God," he said.
"There's nothing He can't do.

"He'll send the Holy Spirit down.
But that's not all God's done.
For though Elizabeth is old,
she, too, will have a son."

And Mary said, "It's wonderful
that I may serve the Lord.
Whatever God wants, I will do
according to His Word."

And when the angel disappear
then Mary packed to go.
"The angel told me what to d
I know where I will go.

"I'll go and see Elizabeth;
it's just the thing to do.
And I would like to know if she
has seen the angel too."

She said, "Good-by," and hurried off.
It was not long before
Elizabeth heard Mary knock.
She hurried to the door.

Elizabeth saw Mary there.
Her heart was filled with joy.
"Great wonders have been done," she said,
"I, too, will have a boy!

"Our God has blessed us both," she said,
"but you're the honored one.
You are the one God chose to be
the mother of His Son."

And Mary sang a song of praise.
"Lord, I believe that You
will send Your Son to save us as
You promised You would do."

That night they sat and talked when there
was nothing else to do.
And Mary said, "I wondered if
you saw the angel too."

Elizabeth said, "No, not I!
He did not come to me!
But Zechariah was the one
the angel came to see.

"An angel suddenly appeared
quite close to where he stood,
and Zechariah shook with fear
as anybody would.

"The angel said, 'Don't be afraid.
I have good news for you.
You know that you are very old
and that your wife is too.

" 'But God has a surprise for you,
a very special one.
Our God decided it is time
to give you both a son.

" 'You'll call him John. He will prepare
the people for God's Son.
He'll baptize men and preach *good news*
and say, "God's Son is come!" ' "

"My husband said, 'How will I know
the things you say are true?'
The sign the angel gave is why
he cannot talk to you."

And Mary stayed with them three months.

But then she said one day,
  "It's time for me to go back home.

I should be on my way."

She said, "Good-by," and hurried home.
When Joseph married her,
he said, "Now we must make our home,
so where would you prefer?"

'Let's stay right here," she said. But God
had other plans for them,
and so He had them leave their home
and go to Bethlehem.

The town was crowded,
rooms were scarce
when they arrived that day.

A stable was the only place
where both of them could stay.

And late that night God's Son was born,
and Jesus was His name.
But everyone in town slept on
and didn't know He came.

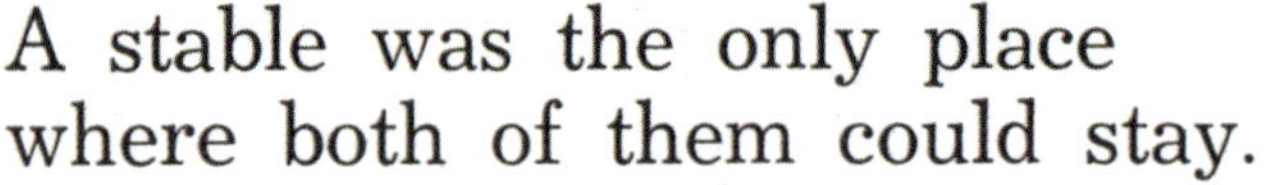

Some shepherds were the first to know.
While tending sheep that night,
an angel suddenly they saw.
The hills were bright with light.

"Don't be afraid," the angel said.
"Just go to Bethlehem,
and you will find your Savior there.
Now go and worship Him."

"He's come!" one said. "The Savior whom
we've waited for is here!"
"Let's go and see!" another said.
"That town is very near."

More angels came to them before
they went to Bethlehem.
"Glory be to God on high!"
the angels sang to them.

"Peace on earth! Goodwill to men!
God's Son has come to earth!"
After that they went and found
the place of Jesus' birth.

They found the stable where He was
and quietly went in
to worship Jesus, who had come
to save us from our sin.

Dear Parents:

The birth of Jesus is the central point of the familiar Christmas Gospel, but St. Luke tells us that some wonderful things happened before He was born in the stable in Bethlehem.

The angel messenger paid a surprise visit to the maiden Mary and announced that she would bear the promised Son. When she questioned how this could be, the angel gave the answer: The Holy Spirit would come and make it possible for her to conceive, for God can do anything. In childlike faith young Mary accepted the Word of the Lord and promised to be His servant.

Bursting to share the news, she hurried to visit her cousin Elizabeth. Can you imagine their excitement as they discussed the wonders of God? Elizabeth would become the mother of John the Baptist, and Mary would give birth to the promised Savior.

Will you help your child see the wonder of God's grace in choosing a humble maid to be the mother of Jesus? Will you lead him to see the joy of Mary in believing the Word of God and in doing what He asked? Above all, will you share the Good News that Jesus Christ is born to take away evil and to make us happy children of God?

THE EDITOR

QUALITY RELIGIOUS BOOKS FOR CHILDREN
ARCH BOOKS
DONKEY DANIEL
in Bethlehem

DONKEY
DANIEL
in Bethlehem

LUKE 2:1-18 FOR CHILDREN

Written by
Janice Kramer

Illustrated by
Obata Design Inc.
Alice Hauser

Nearby the town of Nazareth,
a long, long time ago,
there lived a little donkey
with a nose as white as snow.

His name was Donkey Daniel.
He was very strong indeed;
why, he could carry anything
that anyone might need.

He loved his master Joseph,
 who was gentle as could be.

He loved his cozy, little stall. He loved his favorite tree.

But
Donkey Daniel
had a wish,
a wish he somehow knew
had very, very little chance
of ever coming true.

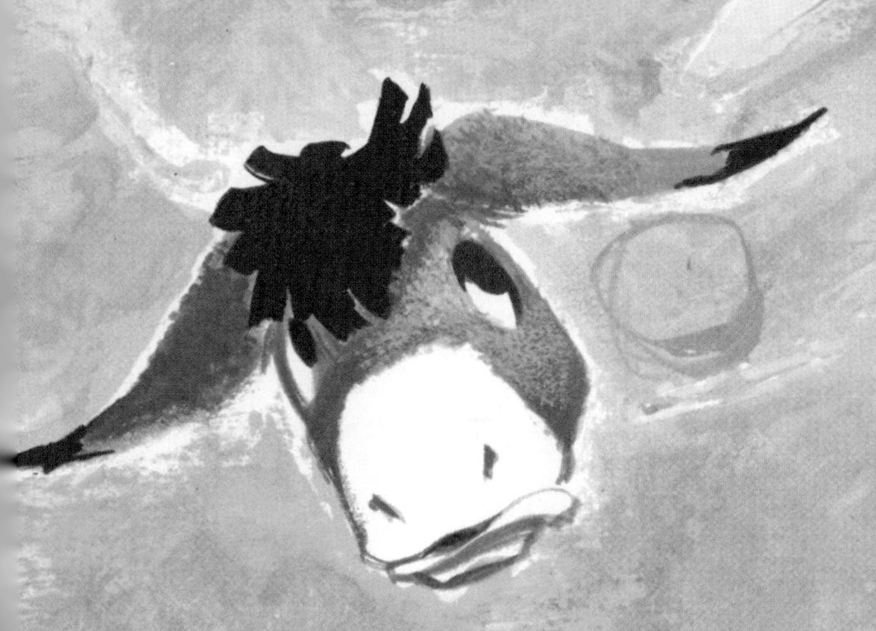

He wanted so to see the world,
to learn what lay beyond
the fences of his master's yard,
the neighbor's muddy pond.

"Perhaps behind those
distant hills," he thought,
"the sky is brown.
Perhaps the grass is pink.
Perhaps the trees grow upside down."

One morning master Joseph came
to Donkey Daniel's stall.
"I've brought your breakfast," Joseph said.
"Be sure to eat it all.

Today we leave for Bethlehem,
and you must come along
to bring some things and carry Mary
on your back so strong."

"I'm going to go
to Bethlehem!"
thought Donkey Daniel.
"Whee!
Oh, now I'll learn about the world!
Oh, now I'll get to see!"

He stood impatiently as Joseph
started in to pack
the things he'd have to carry
on his sturdy little back.

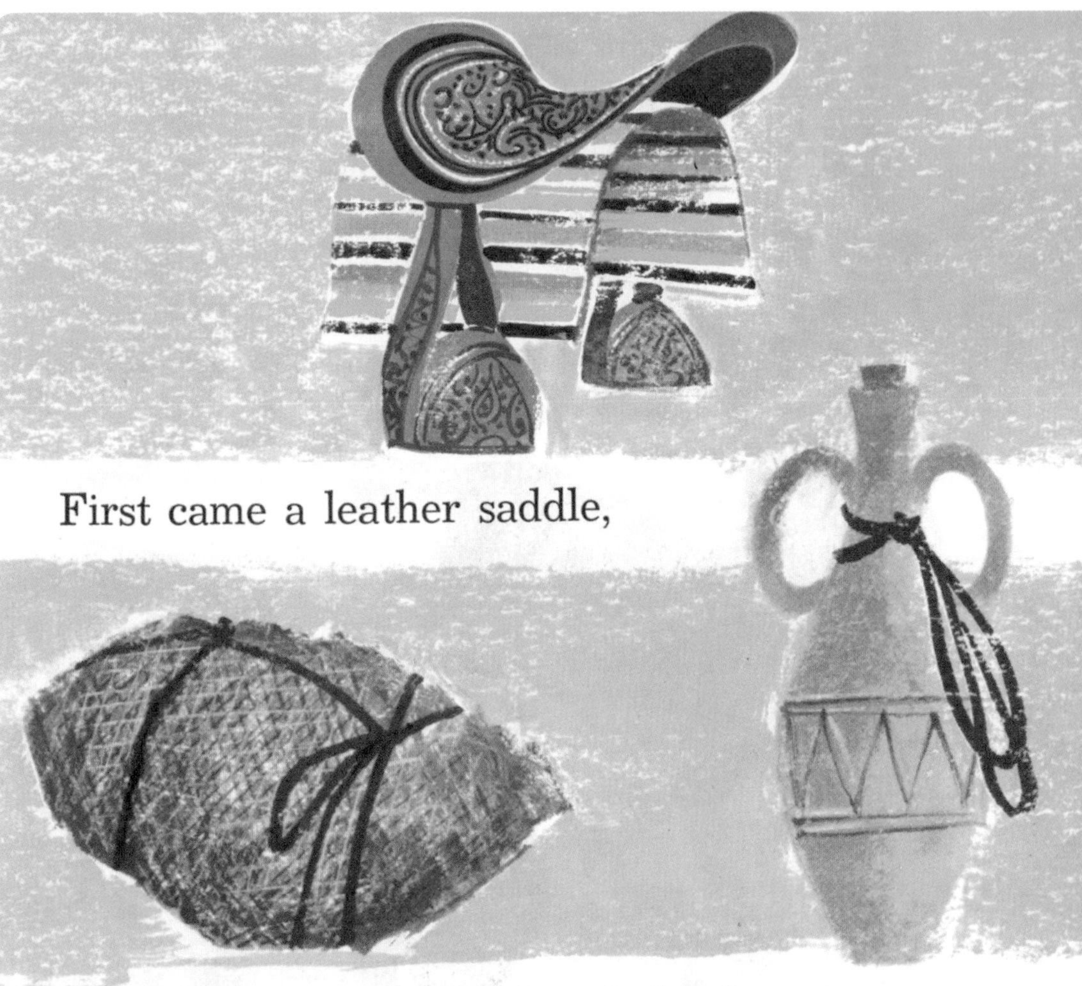

First came a leather saddle,

then some bags of food and drink,

and a tiny sack of money—
he could hear the coins go "clink!"

Then Joseph lifted Mary up.
She seemed so very small
that Donkey Daniel hardly felt
her on his back at all.

"It's time for us to go," said Joseph.
"I will walk ahead."
And Donkey Daniel followed
where his gentle master led.

They passed the houses and the wall,
right out of town they went.
And when they reached the distant hills,
they started their ascent.

Straight up they climbed,
till Donkey Daniel
thought they'd hit the sky.
"Why, I can see
for miles around!"
he cried.
"Oh, my!
OH, MY!"

Then down they went, through valleys green,
past laughing little streams.
"The real world," Donkey Daniel thought,
"is better than my dreams."

They walked and walked for days,
and then, at last, one afternoon,
good Joseph cried, "There's Bethlehem!
We ought to be there soon!"

"That is good news!" said Mary.
Oh, how gladly she replied,
for she was very tired
from the long and bumpy ride.

The town of Bethlehem was filled
with visitors that day,
so Joseph had to look and look
to find a place to stay.

But no one had an empty room,
and so they had to sleep
on hay inside a stable filled
with chickens, cows, and sheep.

They ate their supper,
   made their beds,
      and shut the stable door.
Then Mary fell asleep, and Joseph
      started in to snore.

"Good night," said Donkey Daniel
    to the chickens, cows, and sheep.
    Soon all was calm and silent.
    Everyone was fast asleep.

But Donkey Daniel wakened
in the middle of the night.
"How strange!" he mumbled.
"Mary's up. The stable's filled with light.

And Joseph, why is he awake?
Whatever can it be?
        I must find out what's going on.
        I must get up and see!"

He didn't quite expect to see
the sight that met his eyes.
"A BABY!" Donkey Daniel cried,
with wonder and surprise.

"Why, Mary's had a baby boy,
         and such a lovely child!
See there!
         He looked at me just then.
I think He even smiled!"

Then suddenly a knock was heard
upon the stable door.
Three men came in, quite out of breath,
and knelt upon the floor.

"We're shepherds,"
they explained.
"We've come to see the Son of God!"
"What do they mean?"
thought Donkey Daniel.
"This is very odd."

He tried to understand each word
        the happy shepherds said:
how angels had appeared to say
        that in a manger bed
they'd find the Son of God, a Child
        newborn of holy birth,
a Baby who was Christ the Lord,
        the Savior of the earth!

He tried but didn't understand
        the many words he heard.
How could a tiny, little babe
        be Christ, the mighty Lord?
But then a strange thing happened:
        something made him bow his head
before the Baby Jesus lying in the manger bed.

DEAR PARENTS:

The imaginary Donkey Daniel longs to see the great sights. His wish is to travel beyond his little world in the village of Nazareth.

His wish is finally fulfilled. He sees many new sights on the way to Bethlehem, but the greatest sight is a surprise. He sees the promised Savior, Christ the Lord, a newborn Child.

Like the donkey, many children and adults want to see the world. The ancients wrote about the seven great wonders of the world. In these days of air and space travel many have their travel dreams fulfilled. It is a thrilling adventure to see many natural and manmade wonders in strange and distant places.

As our story shows, the greatest wonder of all is the coming of God in the form and flesh of a human Child. This is the "great and mighty wonder" we sing about in our Christmas hymns and carols.

Our story ends with Donkey Daniel bowing his head before the Child Jesus in the manger. This reflects the tradition in stories and carols that "ox and ass before Him bow," that even animals and nature recognized the mystery that in the Child of Mary God is made manifest in the flesh.

We hope our story will appeal to the imagination of your child. Use it to point to the true meaning of Christmas, that the Son of God came as a humble Child to share our lives, to take our sin and suffering on Himself, and to give Himself on the cross for our forgiveness.

THE EDITOR

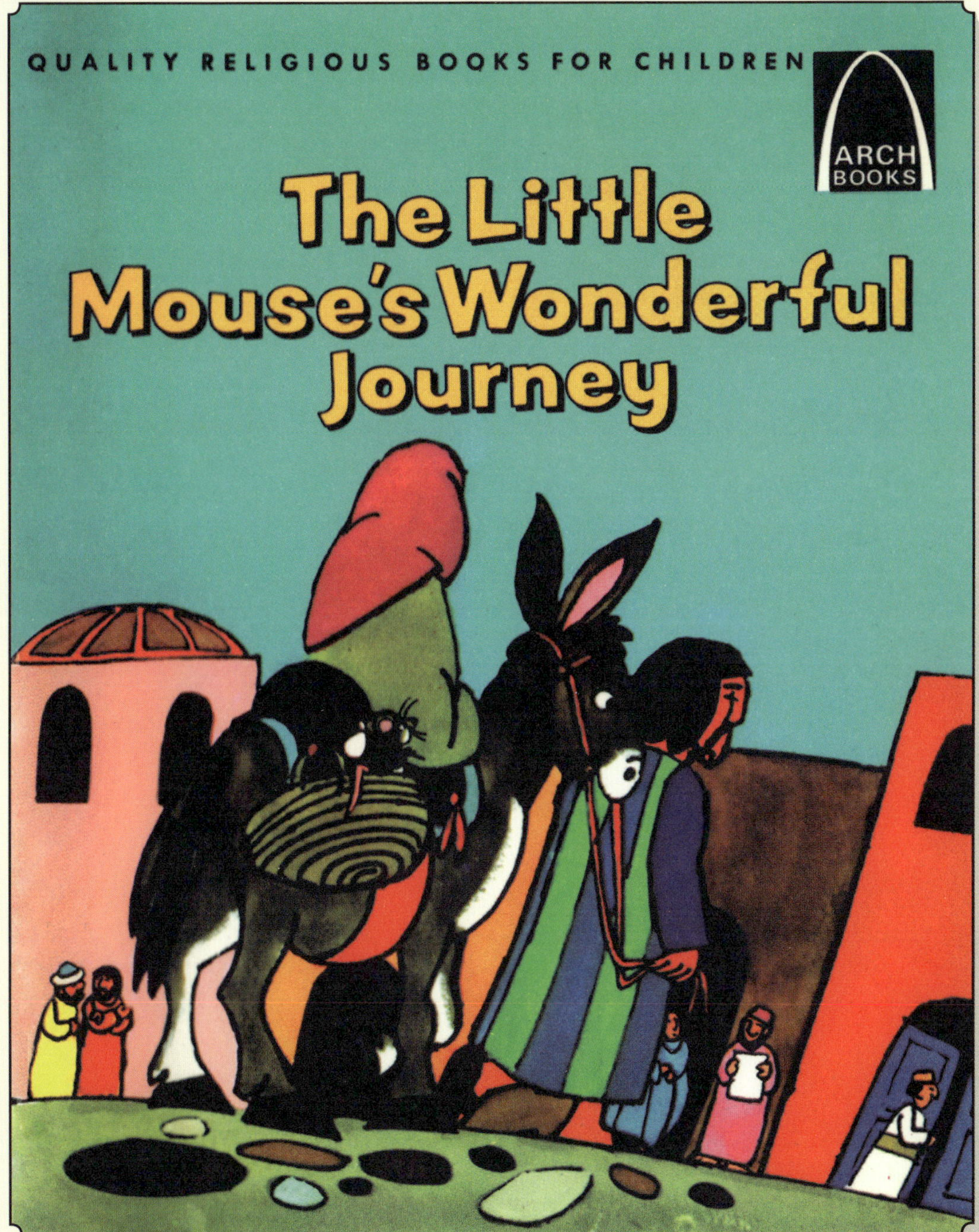
QUALITY RELIGIOUS BOOKS FOR CHILDREN
ARCH BOOKS
The Little Mouse's Wonderful Journey

The Little Mouse's Wonderful Journey

Concordia Publishing House

ARCH Books

COPYRIGHT © 1972 CONCORDIA PUBLISHING HOUSE, ST. LOUIS, MISSOURI

CONCORDIA PUBLISHING HOUSE LTD., LONDON, E. C. 1

MANUFACTURED IN THE UNITED STATES OF AMERICA

ALL RIGHTS RESERVED

ISBN 0-570-06069-9

Clip-Clop was a donkey,
and Timmy was a mouse.
The little barn they lived in
was back of Mary's house.

Mary was a gentle girl
and not afraid of mice;
she left him honeycake to eat
and other things as nice.

One morning Timmy lay asleep
on some of Clip-Clop's straw —
eyes tightly shut, mouth open wide,
his head upon one paw.

While dreaming he heard Clip-Clop bray,
"Hee-haw! Hee-haw! Hee-haw!"
Then Timmy opened up his eyes,
surprised at what he saw.

Clip-Clop had his saddle on,
ready for a trip;
his bellyband was pulled quite tight,
so that it wouldn't slip.

"Where are you going?" Timmy asked.
"I don't know," Clip-Clop replied.
"But see that basket on the ground?
Why don't you get inside?

"No matter where I'm going,
I would like to have you along.
Besides, you weigh almost nothing at all,
while I am big and strong."

So Timmy did as Clip-Clop said,
and the basket soon was tied,
along with clothes and other things,
tightly to Clip-Clop's side.

Then Joseph, Mary's husband, said,
"Let's not forget the food.
That's all!" he cried. "We're ready!
Everything looks good!"

They traveled several days and nights
past hills and woods and streams
to a city much more wonderful
than Timmy's wildest dreams.

The city was full of people!
There were people everywhere!
There were crowds and crowds of people —
all Timmy could do was stare.

"What is the name of this city?
Where have you brought little me?"
"I'm not too sure of it," said Clip-Clop,
"But I know it begins with 'B.'"

Now, the city was so filled with people
that no place to sleep could be found,
and poor Mary and Joseph walked everywhere,
around and around and around.

At last they found an innkeeper,
with a long, white beard on his chin,
who said, "I'm sorry to tell you,
there is no room in my inn.

"But if you are not too fussy,
I do believe I am able
(for a very small sum of money)
to let you sleep in the stable."

Now Mary and Joseph were tired,
and Timmy was tired too.
They went to the stable and opened the door,
and the first thing they heard was a "MOO!"

There were cows in the stable, and donkeys and goa
and noisy geese and white sheep.
But in spite of the noise they laid themselves down,
and in minutes they all were asleep.

All but Timm

Timmy did not like the noise.
"I'll go outside," he said,
"and find a nice, soft clump of grass
and use that for a bed."

He crept outside and down the street
and trotted out of town.
He ran through fields and up a hill
and finally lay down.

Timmy soon fell fast asleep,
his head upon one paw.
Then suddenly he woke again,
surprised at what he saw.

Shepherds all around him stood;
the sky was filled with light,
and a voice said, "Christ the Savior
has been born this very night!"

The shepherds then all hurried off
as fast as they were able
and Timmy followed, surprised to find
they led him to the stable.

The shepherds knelt before a Child
and said: "This wondrous light
is the same light we saw shining
in the fields tonight.

"This blessed Child is surely Christ,
the Son of God," they said.
"How strange the King, our Lord, has but
a manger for a bed!"

Then Mary glanced at Timmy,
who had come in from the street,
and saw the little mouse from home
between dear Clip-Clop's feet.

She smiled at him, and Timmy said:
"Oh, Clip-Clop, I'm so glad
you brought me on this lovely trip,
the best I ever had!"

DEAR PARENTS:

Christmas is for the animal world too. It is a happy part of the world of children — and fantasy can convey many a meaningful thought to the child.

Think of a story like this one as a kind of parable. Let the little mouse help your child to identify with the small and beloved creatures as they bask in the dazzling wonder of the Savior's birth. For the love that Jesus brings to the world is meant to spread from the blessed children of God also to His animal world.

There is another lesson in this story. As the animals render joyful praise and willing service to their Lord by instinct, God's children can do so by choice. And this is the kind of love that means so much to Him.

Let that Christmas Eve, when even the animals and stones could hardly keep from singing, inspire your child to make up his own story in which he is the main character who arrives in his own way at the manger in wonder and joy.

THE EDITOR

QUALITY RELIGIOUS BOOKS FOR CHILDREN
ARCH BOOKS
THE BABY BORN IN A STABLE

THE BABY BORN IN A STABLE

LUKE 2:1-18 FOR CHILDREN

Written by Janice Kramer

Illustrated by Dorse Lampher

Concordia Publishing House

Not quite two thousand years ago
the emperor decreed
that all the world must be enrolled....
LET NO ONE FAIL TO HEED.

(The world was quite mixed up, you see,
and no one seemed to know:
how many people WERE there? And
what taxes did they owe?)

Throughout the earth the rich,
the poor, the young, the very old,
all traveled to their towns of birth
so they could be enrolled.

And so it was, to Bethlehem
a man named Joseph went
to list his name and see how much
he owed the government.
Beside him Mary traveled, too.
Not once did she protest
how long and hard the trip had been,
how much she needed rest.

In Bethlehem they found the inn
and knocked upon the door.
"My rooms are filled!" the owner yelled,
"I haven't any more!"
When Joseph told him quietly
of gentle Mary's plight:
that she would have a baby soon,
perhaps that very night,

the owner stood in thought and rubbed
his bushy bearded jaw.
"I'll let you have the stable, then.
You'll have to sleep on straw."

So Joseph and his wife unpacked
and settled down to rest
not caring that they couldn't have
the biggest and the best.
They ate their supper slowly as
they watched the sun go down,
and yawned as darkness fell at last
upon the little town.

The night was silent. Everyone,
it seemed, was fast asleep
except for shepherds in the fields
who had to watch their sheep.
They huddled close and whispered low
to keep themselves awake.

Then suddenly their eyes grew wide —
their knees began to shake.
For there, above them in the sky,
an angel did appear.
The glory of the Lord shone down,
and they were filled with fear.

The angel spoke: "Fear not! Behold,
I bring you news of joy!
In Bethlehem this very night
was born a baby boy
who is the Savior, Christ the Lord;
He'll win over death and sin.
Upon a manger bed He lies,
behind a lowly inn."

And suddenly a multitude
of angels filled the sky,
their voices glorifying God
and praising Him on high!
And "*Peace on earth, good will to men!*"
resounded through the air —
it seemed there must have been at least
a million angels there!

No longer did the shepherds quake
with anxious fear and dread,
and when the angels disappeared
the shepherds quickly said:
"Oh, let us go to Bethlehem
and find the manger bed!"
And off across the fields they ran —
to Bethlehem they sped!

The manger wasn't hard to find,
and there the shepherds' eyes
fell on a sight that filled their hearts
with wonder and surprise:

For there was Joseph, standing tall
and gazing down with care
upon his blessed Mary and
the baby lying there.

"A wondrous child!" the shepherds cried
in voices of delight.
"See there — around him shines a strange
and heav'nly looking light.
How warm and bright it seems against
the coldness of this night!
He surely is the one we seek;
the angel's words were right!"

To Mary and to Joseph and
to everyone they saw
the shepherds told the story that
had filled them with such awe:
"This baby is the Promised Prince,
        the Mighty Lord,
        the King.

We know because tonight we heard
the holy angels sing.
They told us that this blessed child
of low and humble birth
was truly Christ, the Son of God,
the Savior of the earth!"

The news was spread from town
to town.

The whole world must be told
till every person,

rich

has heard about the coming of
the Savior of all men,
whom God has sent to earth because
of His great love for them.

A CHILD'S CHRISTMAS PRAYER

Be near me, Lord Jesus;

I ask Thee to stay

close by me forever,

and love me, I pray.

Bless all the dear children

in Thy tender care,

and take us to heaven

to live with Thee there.

DEAR PARENTS:

Have you ever had the feeling that your child is confused at Christmastime? There is such a mixture of reindeer, Santa Claus, presents, parties, angels, and unreal mangers. What are we really celebrating, and why? How did it all happen?

Our book is intended to help parents and children remember the real story of the first Christmas and the love of God behind it. Our heavenly Father sent us a Savior who did not shrink from being poor and unrecognized. Christ wasn't even born in a house. We often forget this and tend to be too romantic about the manger in the stable. Mary and Joseph had a hard time of it! The shepherds who welcomed the Christ Child were the nobodies of society in that day. Our God chooses hard and strange ways to win back His children. This is why Jesus came. He saves us from the power of sin and brings God's life back to us.

This is the Good News, and really the only reason we celebrate Christmas. Without it we would have only empty trimmings. Will you help your child see the heart of Christmas by making the first Christmas come alive for him and by centering the season in the birth of Christ?

THE EDITOR

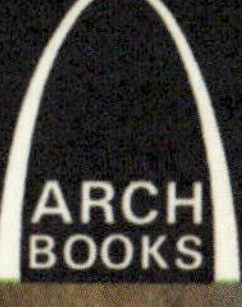

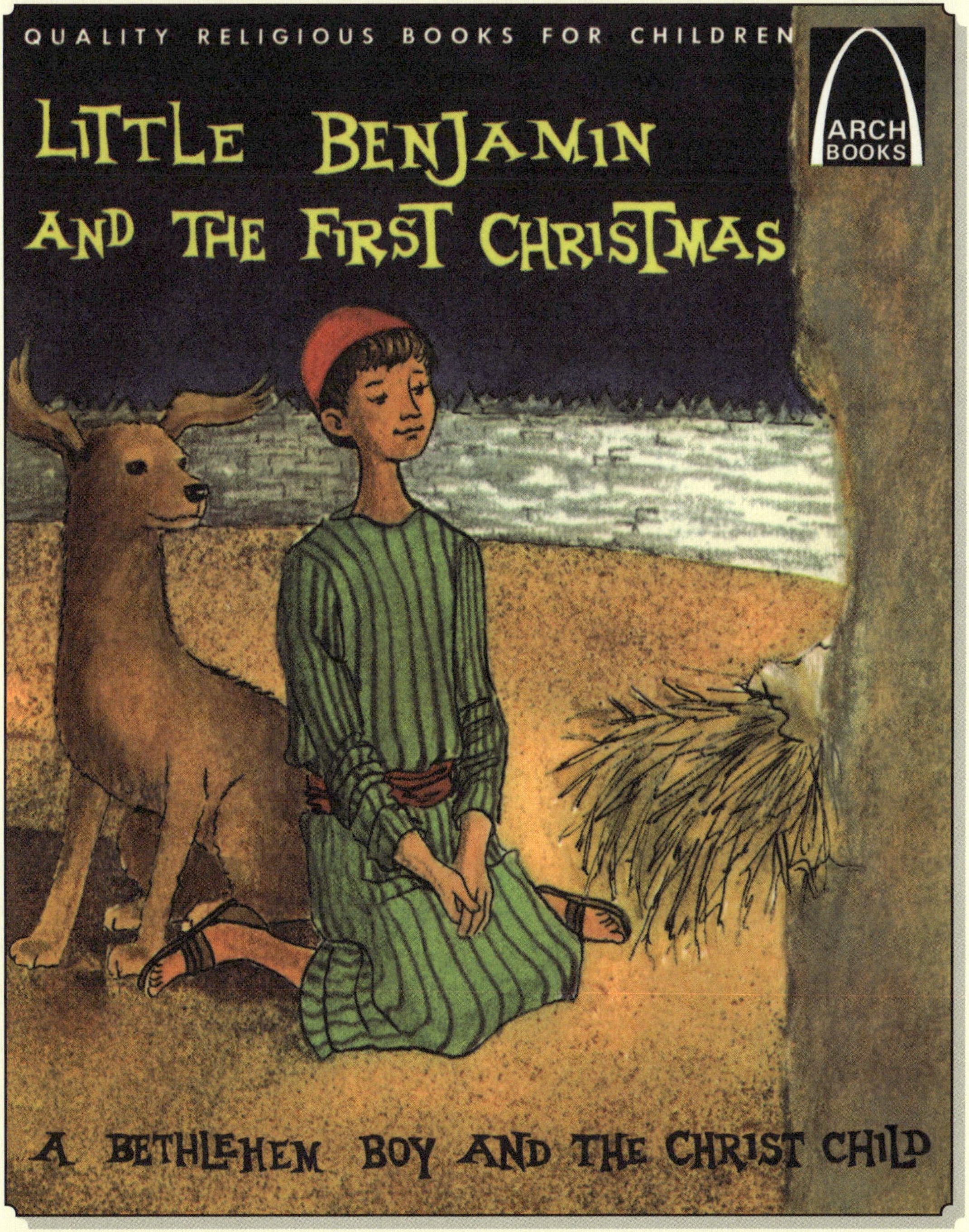
QUALITY RELIGIOUS BOOKS FOR CHILDREN
ARCH BOOKS
LITTLE BENJAMIN AND THE FIRST CHRISTMAS
A BETHLEHEM BOY AND THE CHRIST CHILD

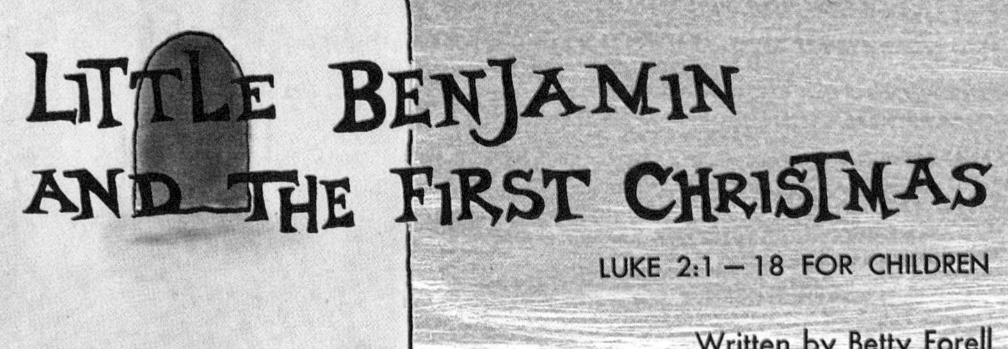

LITTLE BENJAMIN AND THE FIRST CHRISTMAS

LUKE 2:1 — 18 FOR CHILDREN

Written by Betty Forell

Illustrated by Betty Wind

Concordia Publishing House
St. Louis, Missouri

Benjamin watched the people coming into Bethlehem. What a lot of people there were! The king had ordered them to come to Bethlehem to be counted.

Some of them stayed in Benjamin's father's inn. Soon all the rooms were taken.

The inn was full of noise and excitement. "Here, boy, bring some hay for our donkeys!" they called out to Benjamin.

Finally Father locked the gate. No more room. Not even a corner. The family was tired and hungry. Supper smelled good. Father led them in their evening prayers. He read from the great prophet Isaiah:

"The people who walked in darkness have seen a great light. . . . For to us a Child is born. . . . , the Prince of Peace."

Father told the children what the words meant. "God has promised to send us a very special Prince to rule over all people and save us from wars and bad kings. In His kingdom all people will live together in love and peace."

"When will this Prince come?" Benjamin sighed. "This is such an old promise from God. Will it ever come true? Will I ever get to see the wonderful Prince?"

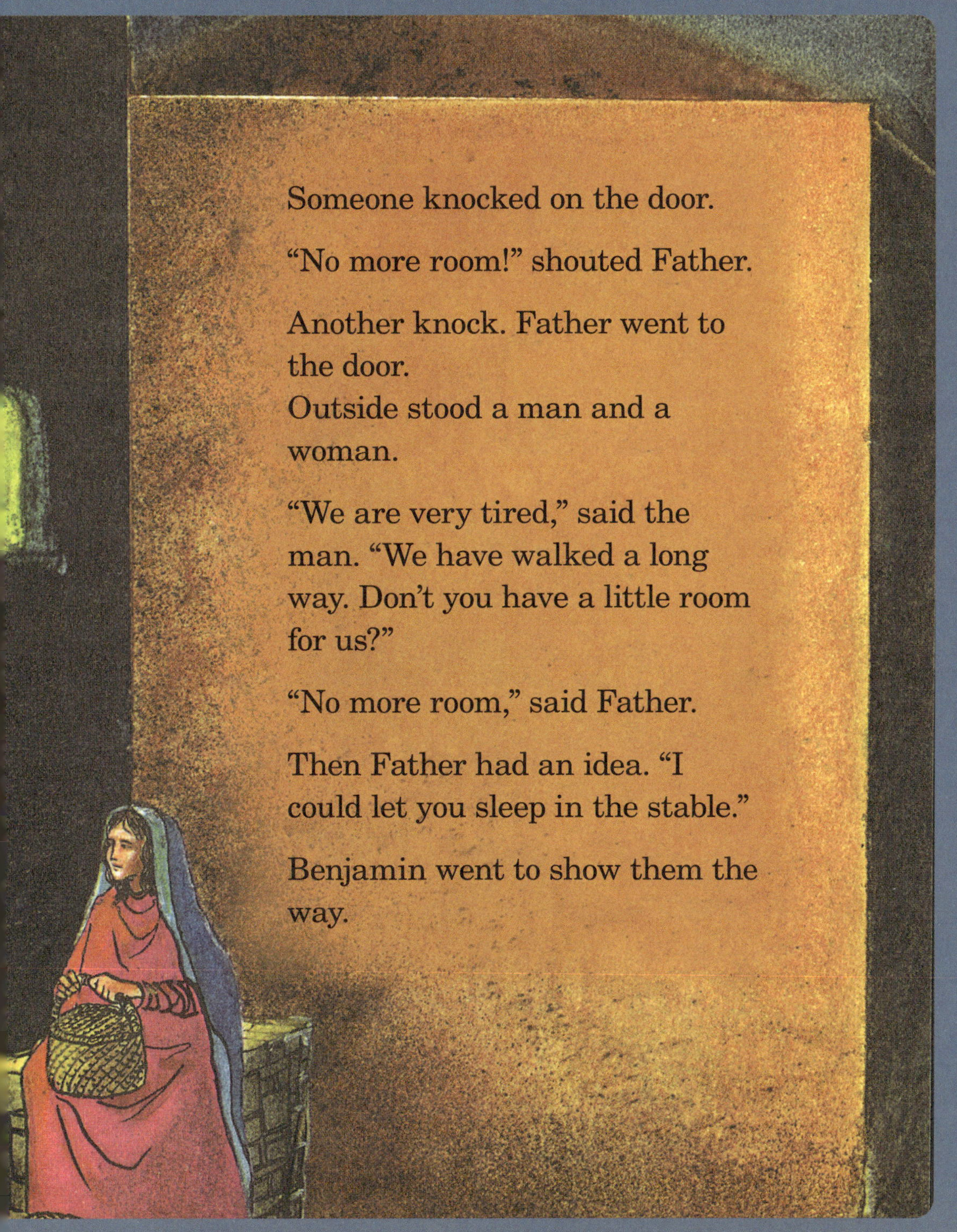

Someone knocked on the door.

"No more room!" shouted Father.

Another knock. Father went to the door.
Outside stood a man and a woman.

"We are very tired," said the man. "We have walked a long way. Don't you have a little room for us?"

"No more room," said Father.

Then Father had an idea. "I could let you sleep in the stable."

Benjamin went to show them the way.

Through the courtyard he guided them, past sleepy travelers, to the stable.

The animals in the stable looked up as they came
in and watched Benjamin pile fresh hay in a
corner for the man and woman to sleep on.

"'What's your name?" the man asked him.

"Benjamin," he answered.

"My name is Joseph," said the man, "and this is Mary, my wife. It took us five days to get here from Nazareth on foot."

Soon the town quieted down. The weary visitors and the tired townspeople all slept.

Benjamin was dreaming of all the crowds he had seen that day.

Suddenly, something awakened him. He ran to the window. A very bright star was rising in the sky. Everything was quiet except for the cry of a baby. But there was a light in the stable. Benjamin rubbed his eyes. Were there people going into the stable?

In a flash Benjamin slipped out of the room, out of the inn, out to the stable. There he saw an amazing sight.

On the hay which Benjamin himself
had put in the manger for the animals, lay a beautiful, newborn baby.
Mary and Joseph were watching
over the baby. And close by knelt a
group of shepherds.

"What are those shepherds doing here?" Benjamin asked himself. "And why are they kneeling?"

One of the shepherds beckoned to him.
The shepherd was a rough looking fellow. Benjamin was just a bit afraid of
him.

But the man said, "Come in and see! It's the Prince of Peace!" The man's voice was so full of wonder that Benjamin forgot his fear.

"A Prince?" Benjamin asked. "But He's just a baby and in a stable."

"As we were watching our sheep tonight" the shepher
said, "suddenly an angel came to us. We were terribl
frightened. But then the angel said:

'Be not afraid . . . I bring you good news . . . for to you is born this day in the city of David a Savior, who is Christ the Lord. And this will be a sign for you: you will find a Babe . . . lying in a manger.'

"Then came many more angels, all singing praise to God."

As soon as they went away, we went and found this stable. Here is the Baby in a manger just as the angel said!"

So this Baby was the Savior, the Prince
of Peace for whom Benjamin and his
father and his grandfather and his great-
grandfather had waited all these years.
Benjamin stepped forward to see the
little Christ Child better.

Then he knelt down. He thought of
what his father had read that evening:

"The people who walked in darkness
have seen a great light. . . . For to us a
Child is born . . . the Prince of Peace."

Dear Parents:

The story tries to tell about the coming of the Christ Child the way a small Jewish boy of Jesus' time would have seen it. It tries to show how very much and why he would have been waiting for it. It reminds us how he would have been surprised to see the great Prince Messiah, the Lord Christ, as a baby in the place where he put food each day for the domestic animals.

By and large the people of Jesus' day expected the Messiah, or the Lord Christ, to come with kingly power and glory. His coming as their humble brother went against all they had expected. God's ways are so different from ours.

One of the promises God made about the Messiah was that His would be a kingdom with true peace between men, nature, and God (Is. 9:6, 7; 11:1-10). There was no agreement among the Jewish people how this would come about. The New Testament sees the peace which God offers in Jesus Christ as the coming of the Messiah's kingdom of peace and the brotherly love in Christ's church as part of it. When Jesus returns in glory, all evil will be destroyed. Then the dream of Benjamin and of his father and grandfather will come true.

Can you help your child to see the true meaning of Christmas, with its wonder over the love of God which made the Lord Christ want to share the humblest and commonest way of life, the love which brings peace from God and makes peace among men possible? You may want to read to your child (or help him read it himself) the story of Jesus' birth in your Bible. (Luke 2:1-20)

The Editor

QUALITY RELIGIOUS BOOKS FOR CHILDREN
14 ARCH BOOKS
the man who didn't have time

THE CHRISTMAS STORY FOR CHILDREN

Written by Yvonne Holloway McCall
Illustrated by Betty Wind

ARCH Books
Copyright © 1976 CONCORDIA PUBLISHING HOUSE, ST. LOUIS, MISSOURI
MANUFACTURED IN THE UNITED STATES OF AMERICA
ALL RIGHTS RESERVED
ISBN 0-570-06112-1

The innkeeper rushed.
He was in such a hurry.
All he had time for was money and worry.
In his little hotel
The nooks and the crannies
Were jammed full of children,
And parents and grannies.
He growled as he answered
A knock on the door.
He didn't have room for anyone more.

He peered at a man in the shadowy light
And a woman and donkey alone in the night.

"My wife," said the man, "is weary and worn
For you see, her baby's about to be born."
"No room," the busy innkeeper said.
And he showed it was so
By a shake of his head.

"I'm sorry. I'd like to help and be kind,
But I simply have too much else on my mind.
Although," he mused,
"In the barn you could stay.
It's there in the back, out of the way.
It isn't exactly a first-class hotel.
There are flies and dirt,
And the animals smell,

But take it or leave it.
It's all that I've got."
And the man in the shadows
Sighed at the thought.
But he went and made pillows
Of hay in the stable
For Mary, his wife, as best he was able.

And the innkeeper went
To his own cozy suite
And then made sure he had plenty to eat.

Then he went back to working
As fast as he could
And did all the things
That an innkeeper should.

And shepherds were working
A night shift, as well,
When an angel appeared
With a story to tell.
He stood in their midst
In a shimmering light,
And their hearts started jumping
And thumping with fright.

The angel announced, "I bring you the news
That the Savior's been born,
The King of the Jews.
You'll find Him wrapped up,
In a manger of hay."
And the shepherds all turned
To each other to say,

"Come on, let's go just as fast as we can."
And they dropped all their work
In the field and ran.

Oh, how delighted they were when they saw
The Baby, their King, asleep in the straw.
Their hearts were merry.
They bubbled with mirth.
And the news started spreading
All over the earth—

While the man at the inn
Kept working so hard
He missed what happened
In his own backyard.
But . . .

n the sky in the East,
n a far distant land,
God hung a star, brilliant and grand.

Three Wise Men said,
"It's to tell us the news
That a Savior's been born,
The King of the Jews."

They stopped and dropped
All the work they were doing,
For something of far more
Importance was brewing.

They loaded camels with treasures and gold
And all the supplies
That their saddles could hold.
Through hot, sandy deserts
They traveled each day.
The star was a compass to show the way.
Their friends and families
Were all left behind.

For months they continued,
One purpose in mind.

To them the very most wonderful thing
Was to worship the Baby,
Their Savior and King.

And then came a day they rounded the bend
That brought them with joy
To their journey's end.
As they bowed to the Child sent from above,
They gave Him their treasures.
They gave Him their love.

And Wise Men and shepherds
Had peace untold.
They had found God's Gift
More precious than gold.
All of them acted exactly the same.
They pushed aside
Everything else and came.

And the innkeeper? Well . . .
He's a different story.
He missed the peace, the joy and the glory.
He could have said, "Come. Eat at my table.
You take my room. *I'll* take the stable."
But it seems he was hurried
And worried and miffed
And never took time to find God's Gift.

That Gift is Jesus, a Savior, a Friend,
With life forever, that never will end.
He wants to enter your life and your heart
And stay there forever and never depart.

DEAR PARENTS:

Christmas has come to mean many things for each of us. But for most of us Christmas means rushing.

It's the season for rushing around in department and discount stores. It's the time for rushing out to get a tree and a wreath. We rush to get presents wrapped and cookies baked and children dressed for the Christmas program.

At Christmas most of us are the people who don't have time.

The innkeeper in the story was so busy he didn't have time for Jesus either. But the shepherds and Wise Men, when they heard about Jesus' birth, dropped everything and rushed to greet Him. To all people who take time for Him, Jesus gives eternity.

Or, looking at it another way, consider a matter of priorities. If someone knocked on the door with a beautiful gift—a box that contained a most treasured possession—one would certainly not brush him off, close the door, and go busily on with routine activities. Yet that is what many do to God, who holds out a priceless Treasure: peace, joy, forgiveness of sins—all wrapped up in Jesus.

Set aside time this Christmas season to read and discuss this Arch Book with your children. Don't hurry through it. Point out to them the importance of taking time to be with their Lord Jesus, who chose to be with them forever. That's what this story is all about.

THE EDITOR

the innkeeper's daughter

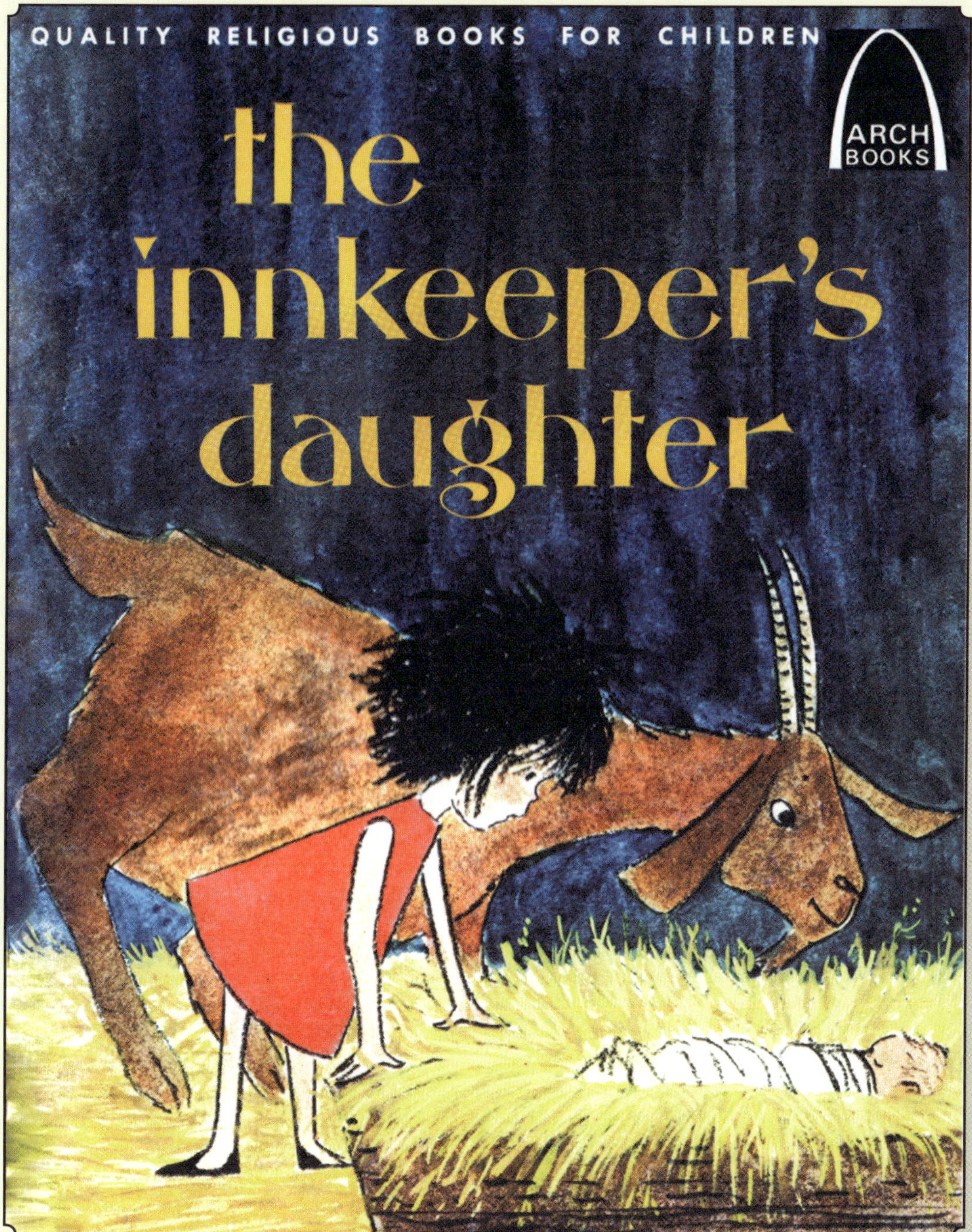

the innkeeper's daughter

Luke 2:1-20 FOR CHILDREN

Written by Carol Greene

Illustrated by Betty Wind

ARCH Books

Copyright © 1973 by Concordia Publishing House, St. Louis, Missouri

Concordia Publishing House Ltd., London, E. C. 1

Manufactured in the United States of America

ISBN 0-570-06077-X

In Bethlehem there lived a girl,
Abigail by name,
And anyplace she showed her face
was never quite the same.

For Abigail was mean as mean,
    a dreadful little girl,
And most of all she loved to put
    the townfolk in a whirl.

She teased their dogs and cats and birds
and set their donkeys free;
She trampled on their flower beds,
stole oranges from their trees;

Made faces at the little kids
    until they cried, and then . . .
She went back where she started from
    and did it all again.

They called her Awful Abigail,
    and really they spoke rightly,
But Abigail just turned her back
    and snickered impolitely.

Her family ran a busy inn,
    but she was rarely there,
For she was usually out someplace
    and into someone's hair.

Her only friend was her pet goat
    —Meangoat was his name—
A raggletaggle bag of fleas
      and not especially tame.

"What shall we do with Abigail?"
    her parents used to moan.
"If she were good, we know she
    wouldn't always be alone."

But only cranky Meangoat
    had ever heard her say,
"And why should I be good when
    no one loves me anyway?"

One day Abigail awoke and
cried out like a banshee,
"I feel *especially* mean today!"
So she got up and then she . . .

Pulled her brother's puppy's tail,
Spilled her mother's garbage pail,

Made her little sister wail.
Awful, *awful* Abigail!

"Go to market, Abigail,"
    her frazzled mother said,
"And bring me back a sack of wheat
    so I can bake some bread."

So Abigail went running off
    with Meangoat close behind,
But still she did each naughty thing
    that popped into her mind.

She . . .
>Scared a baby with a snail,
>Knocked some barley off the scale,
>Yelled that all the cakes were stale.
>Awful, *awful* Abigail!

At last the townfolk chased her home,
and her poor parents said,
"The only thing to do is to
send Abigail to bed.

"With people running in and out,
the inn filled up to bursting,
We can't watch Abigail, and she may
even do a worse thing!"

So off to bed went Abigail, and
    still not one bit sorry,
As evening came, she lay and watched
    the sky turn dark and starry.

"I just don't care!" she said aloud,
    although no one could hear.
"Nobody loves me anyway!"
    But what was that? A tear?

"I will not cry!" said Abigail
    and bounced onto her feet.
"I'll sit here on the windowsill
    and look down at the street."

The night was cold, and down below,
    the street looked dark and bare,
But Abigail thought she heard
    a clopping noise somewhere.

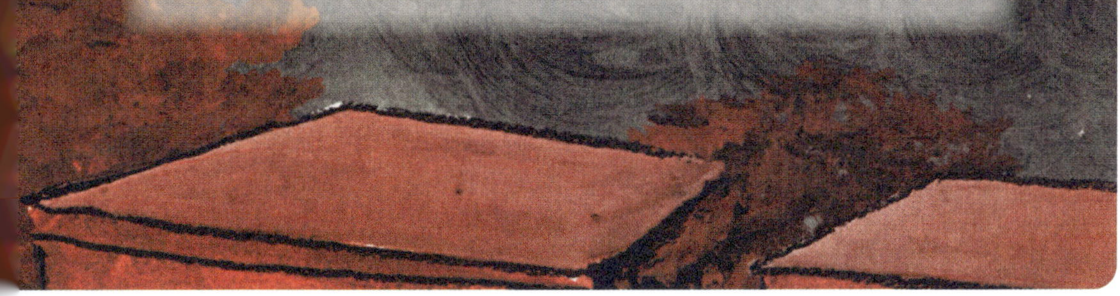

It was a donkey and a couple,
    young and very poor,
Who shivered through the windy street
    and came up to the door.

They knocked, and Abigail's father called,
    "There is no room!"
"Please let us in!" the man implored.
    "Our baby's coming soon!"

The door was opened then,
    and Abigail's father said,
"I wish that I could help you,
    but I've neither room nor bed.

But let me think! I'll do for you
    the one thing I am able.
If you don't mind, just out behind
    the inn you'll find a stable.

It isn't much, but warm and dry
    and better than the street.
Here's what remains from supper too,
    some bread and cheese and meat."

They left with thanks, and Abigail
wondered from her gable
Why God would let these people have
their baby in a stable.

She went to bed and fell asleep,
but not for very long,
For in her dream from far away
she heard an angel's song:

"A wondrous Child is born tonight!
    Let heaven and earth rejoice!"
And wide awake in her small room
    she still could hear that voice.

She slipped into her heavy robe
    and tied her sandals tight,
And, careful not to make a sound,
    she crept into the night.

The stars were bright, and one
    especially hung so very low,
The little stable seemed to gleam
    like silver in its glow.

Up to the door went Abigail,
    but there she paused and said,
"I won't go in. It's late, and they
    all must have gone to bed."

But as she peeked around the door,
    her brown eyes opened wide.
This surely was a miracle,
    the sight she saw inside!

For there on the hay
A new Baby lay;
The animals knelt down beside Him.
His mother's eyes glowed;
The man's happy face showed
The joy that he felt deep inside him.
As Abigail stared,
She felt rather scared
And lost in the wonder around her.
But somehow she knew
A dream had come true
And Someone who loved her had found her.

Just then she felt a dreadful push,
 and through the door she stumbled.
"Oh, Meangoat, why did you do that?"
 she cried, then down she tumbled.

The young man rushed to pick her up
 and brushed her off with care.
"I'm Joseph," he said kindly,
 "And that's Mary over there.

"You're here to see the Child,
    I'm sure. Come closer to the manger.
He's very new, but we know you
    won't cause Him any danger."

"What is His name?" asked Abigail
and touched His little toe.
"Jesus," answered Mary.
"He's a special Child, you know."

"I thought He was," said Abigail.
"But can you tell me why?"
"I think I can," said Mary.
"Here, come sit down, and I'll try.

"He's God's Son, you see;
He's come here to be
A Friend to all people on earth.
God wants us to know
He loves us all, so
He planned this miraculous birth

"The Baby will grow,
And one day He'll show
The world that their sins are forgiven;
And we will be free
To live joyfully
On earth and then later in heaven."

When Abigail at last went back
    and crawled into her bed,
A million happy thoughts all came
    parading through her head.

"This little Baby's come to earth
       to show God loves me too,
And He's forgiven all the
       awful things I used to do.

"But now I know He loves me,
       and so I don't feel mean.
I'll go to sleep and start
       tomorrow absolutely clean!"

       And she did.

Dear Parents:

Abigail was awful—no doubt about it. At one point she tells Meangoat why. Ask the child if he can remember what she said.

Help him see that when *we* feel unloved we tend to be awful too. We may not take our misery out on others to the extent that Abigail did. We may turn it in on ourselves instead. But in either case we're pretty miserable.

Abigail's Christmas realization was that "Someone who loved her had found her." He's found us too. Abigail couldn't have found Him, not alone. Nor could we. But God sent His Son to find us, the Abigails and Ednas and Harrys and Dons—all His lost sheep. That's the glory of Christmas. Once we know we've been found, once we're sure we are loved by Someone who will never stop loving us, the terrible, heartbreaking misery goes away.

Abigail probably didn't stop being awful, at least not completely, even after that first Christmas Eve. We still have our awful moments too. That's the nature of sin. It hangs on and has to be clobbered again and again.

But we don't have to do the clobbering alone. We have the assurance of forgiveness and help from Somone who loves us and has found us—forever.

The Editor

QUALITY RELIGIOUS BOOKS FOR CHILDREN
ARCH BOOKS
THE NIGHT THE ANGELS SANG

THE NIGHT THE ANGELS SANG

Luke 2:8-20 FOR CHILDREN

Written by Allan Ross

Illustrated by Betty Wind

ARCH® Books

COPYRIGHT © 1975 CONCORDIA PUBLISHING HOUSE, ST. LOUIS, MISSOURI

ISBN 0-570-06095-8

Josiah was a shepherd boy
Who lived near Bethlehem.
He helped his father watch the sheep
With other boys and men.

To keep the silly sheep from harm
They had to watch all day,
Then sleep with one eye half awake
To keep the wolves away.

Josiah had a shaggy dog,
Part Hebrew hound, part Greek,
Who ran so fast and jumped so high
The shepherds called him Streak.

Streak helped Josiah herd the sheep;
He kept them all together.
But sometimes just those two went out
For walks in sunny weather.

One day when they were in the hills
They found a little lamb,
An orphan, so they took him home.
They thought they'd call him Sam.

Sam's fleecy coat
        was thick and woolly
And black as
        black could be.

He liked to watch Josiah work
Or Streak hunt for a flea.

One night Josiah and his dad
Were dozing on the hill.
Beside them lay both Sam and Streak.
The night hung dark and still.

Then in the sky there seemed to glow
A faint and moving light.
"Look there!" said Dad. "It's coming close,
A most peculiar sight."

n angel in long flowing
    robes came in view.
siah was worried.
    He covered his eyes.
he light grew much brighter,
    all white mixed with blue.
 a small boy it seemed quite
    a frightening surprise.

"Fear not," said the angel.
        (Streak dived for a bush.)
"You shepherds wake up!
        It's no time for a snooze."
Josiah felt better. He gave Streak a push.
The angel said, "I bring some wonderful news."

"Great joy to all people!" the angel went on.
"For I come to tell that your Savior is born.
In the city of David tonight He has come.
To Bethlehem hurry! You'll be there by morn."

"You'll know when you've found Him—
    now hear what I say—
He's wrapped in soft clothing, asleep in the hay.
The inn was packed tight.
    There was no room at all.
So Mary had Jesus out back in a stall."

With swirling white robes now the sky danced
    and spun.
A heavenly host of bright angels drew near.
And songs of thanksgiving for God's tiny Son
Rang out o'er the hillside,
    rang out glad and clear.

Glory to God in the highest!" they sang.
"And peace on the earth to all men of good will."
Again and again that first Christmas song rang.
Then the angels departed. The night became still.

"Let us go," one shepherd said
—He was the leader of the men—
"To see this thing that's come to pass.
It's not so far to Bethlehem."

"Can I go too?" Josiah asked.
His father thought awhile.
"Well, all right, son," he finally said.
The other shepherds smiled.

"And, Dad, can Streak and Sam go too?
They'll be good. I'll take care.
I'm sure that God won't really mind
If dogs and lambs are there."

His dad agreed, so off they went,
And, as the angels said,
They found the Baby, God's own Son,
Safe in His manger bed.

The shepherds paused and gazed in awe.
A holy feeling o'er them came.

Josiah knelt and closed his eyes.
The other shepherds did the same.

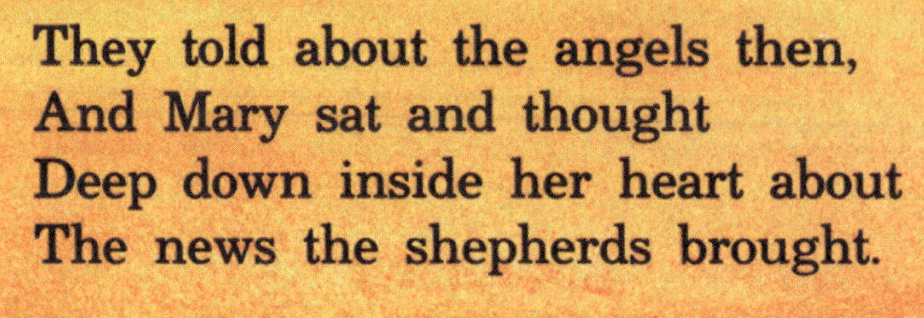

They told about the angels then,
And Mary sat and thought
Deep down inside her heart about
The news the shepherds brought.

At last they left to go back home
But took their time along the way
To tell the people that they met
What happened on that holy day.

They ran and sang and told their news
In voices loud, in voices meek.
And at the very front there ran
Josiah, Sam, and Streak.

Dear Parents:

Imagine yourselves—and ask your children to imagine themselves—as shepherds out on those dark, quiet slopes of the hills above Bethlehem. Your life has been an uneventful one; you rarely even speak to anyone besides your fellow shepherds. And tonight seems to be a night like any other—except perhaps a little colder. You lie with your cloak wrapped snugly around you, drowsing, almost asleep.

Suddenly the sky explodes with light! Before you appears an angel, an angel who announces the most important news ever announced. Then he is joined by a whole choir of angels, who sing the gladdest song ever heard on earth. How can this be happening to you, a mere shepherd, a nobody?

It has happened to you because the news and the song are meant for you and for all people, humble and great. A loving God is speaking to His children—all of them—and His words are wonderful:

"Your Savior is born!

Great joy to all people!"

THE EDITOR

QUALITY RELIGIOUS BOOKS FOR CHILDREN
13
ARCH BOOKS
THE BABY GOD PROMISED

THE BABY GOD PROMISED

Luke 1:26—2:20 FOR CHILDREN

Written by Walter Wangerin Jr.

Illustrated by Bill Heuer

Publishing House
St. Louis

ARCH Books

Mary had a baby.
Mary had a baby.
She named her baby Jesus.
She knew the babe would ease us.
Ah, Mary had a baby boy,
And this is the way that it was.

The angel named Gabriel strolled in her yard
And told her to sit and be still.
"You're special," he said, "in the eyes of the
     Lord,
Handpicked, after He has been looking so hard
For someone to do His good will.

"Maid, you are the garden of God today,
And in you He is planting His seed.
That seed will grow bigger in every way
Until it is born as a boy who will say
That God is His Father indeed!"

Then Mary was staring at this and at that;
"A baby," she whispered so low.
The angel had left her; but there was the cat;
She had to tell someone, and so she said,
    "Cat—
A baby, well what do you know!"

Then Mary was rushing as fast as she could
To tell somebody else the good news:
The baby inside of her had to be good
Since He would be doing what other men
    should.
Oh, she ran! Oh, she wore out her shoes.

Then whom should she go to? And whom did
    she find?
Her kin named Elizabeth;
And when she said "Hi!" to this lady so kind,
Elizabeth shouted, "I just had a sign!
I know why you're out of breath."

Elizabeth giggled, she wiggled her toes;
She grinned and showed all of her teeth.
"A babe is inside of you, I would suppose,
The one Heaven promised, the one Heaven
    chose
To save us from sin and from death!

"Ah, lucky my Mary, and lucky me, too:
You came to *my* kitchen, to *me*!"
And Mary said, "Yes"; she said, "Bessie,
    that's true;
Our Lord has been watching the likes of us
    two,
The lowest there is; but Bessie, we're *His*,
Then how grand and important are we!"

Ah, Mary had a baby, sweet Mary had a boy;
And Heaven said, "You name your joy
Immanuel: He'll know you well."
Good Mary bore a bouncing boy,
And this is the way that it was.

Now, the king in the capital wanted to know
How many his citizens were.
"My people, you pack your baggage and go
To the towns of your mammas and papas,
        and so
I will count you by families there."

Then the people were traveling thither
        and yon—
Grumbling as they passed through the streets;
They shoved and they bustled until they were
        done;
They fussed and they hustled to be the first
        one
To find a hotel with clean sheets.

But Mary moved slowly; round Mary rode
      slow;
She couldn't go faster than that.
See, the baby inside of her — how He did grow!
He was big; He was ready to come, don't you
      know.
So when Mary was tired, she sat.

But Joseph was with her; her husband was
      there,
And he was the kindest of men:
He brought her her water, and he didn't care
If they were the last ones to find the last chair
In the last room in Bethlehem.

Now Mary is groaning, and Joseph is knocking
On every dark door in the night;
But all he can hear is citizens locking
Their doors and their porches. Oh, what is
        more shocking
Than Mary alone and no light?

Poor Mary is groaning: There isn't much
        time;
Her baby is coming so soon.
And Joseph is sweating as bright as a dime,
But "Never mind me," he calls; "I'll help
        you climb
To the stall that I found for a room."

The baby! The baby! Oh, Mary, have your
    Savior.
Dear Mary, bear your boy.
You give Him birth, and men on earth
Shall call Him Christ, Messiah, Worth;
They'll look at each other with joy.

The shepherds are playing at mumblety-peg
For something to do to keep warm,
Are tired and griping with pains in the leg,
And one of them shouting, "Who gobbled
    my egg?
The shepherd who did that, I'll shatter his
    arm!"
These herders know nothing but harm.

Then shepherd and shepherd is hiding his
     head
In his coat like a Halloween hood;
They huddle together like sheep full of dread;
They fear that the weather will soon strike
     them dead—
For a light in the night means no good.

But *this* light is speaking; and this light
     is glory;
For this is an angel on earth.
"Look up," he implores, "and I'll tell you
     a story
More happy than any that you've heard before
     me.
Shepherds, there's just been a birth!

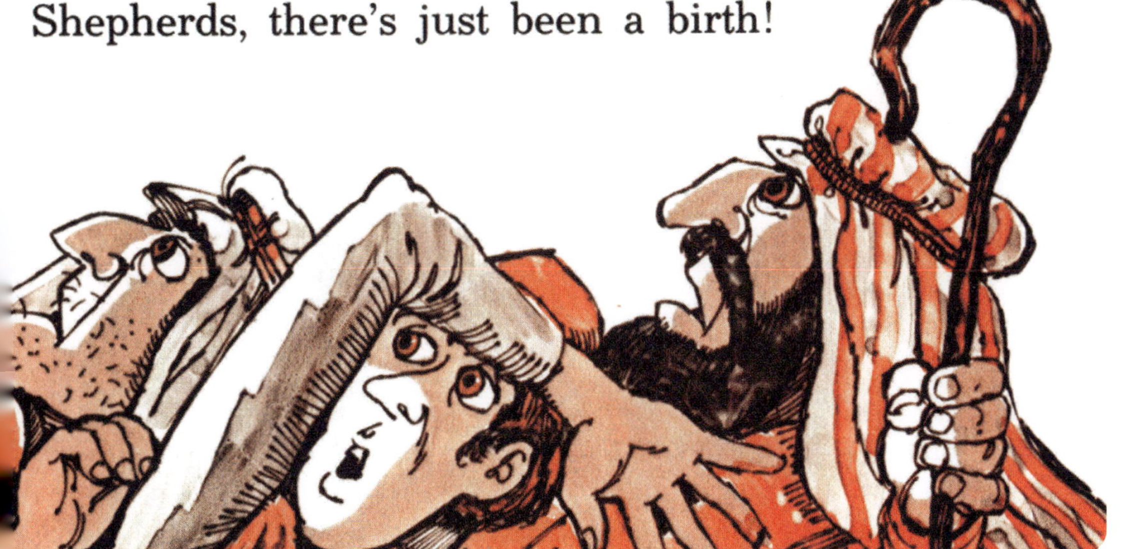

"Jesus, the Savior, your Christ and your Lord
Has been born on this night, this good night!
He waits in a manger; His pillow's a board;
His clothes are but bunting, BUT HE IS
        YOUR LORD!"
Then millions of angels are everywhere
        soaring,
And here and there, everywhere, angels are
        roaring
That God in His glory, that God is now
        pouring
His peace on mankind and His might!

Hush Shepherds, be quiet. Oh, Shepherds, be
    still;
The night is a calm one again.
You stare at each other, you stare at the hill
Where the angels were singing. You know
    God's good will:
Get up. Go to Bethlehem.

And there is His father, and there is His
    mother,
And there is the baby, the boy.
And here are the shepherds in love with
    each other,
For what are they now? They are brother and
    brother
Because of this baby, their joy.

So Mary had a baby
And Mary bore a brilliant child.
His name is Most High; and because of Him I,
And heaven, and everyone smiled.

DEAR PARENTS:

This retelling of the Christmas story emphasizes the gradually growing ripples of light that our Lord's birth brought with it. Christ comes to earth as a seed of light planted in Mary's womb and grows to the "brilliant child" who enlightens the face of heaven itself, and causes us all to smile.

At the same time, the amazing ordinariness of the events is emphasized. Jesus came into the lives of real people, not just of characters in somebody's myth. So the narration combines the two elements of the incarnation: the glory of the Lord and the human situation that glory entered.

Help your chiid discover all the ordinary things in the story, e. g., Elizabeth's teeth, Mary's cat, Joseph's sweaty face as shiny as a dime. Then trace through the story what we might call our sinful situation, e. g., the crowds, the pain, the tired, griping shepherds, etc. Finally, discover with your children how the light Jesus brought gradually grows from a little seed to the great light of the angels in the sky to the glorious radiance of our redemption.

Perhaps you can summarize with something like, "At Christmas Jesus came from heaven into our world and brought with Him His beautiful smile so that now we all can smile too."

THE EDITOR

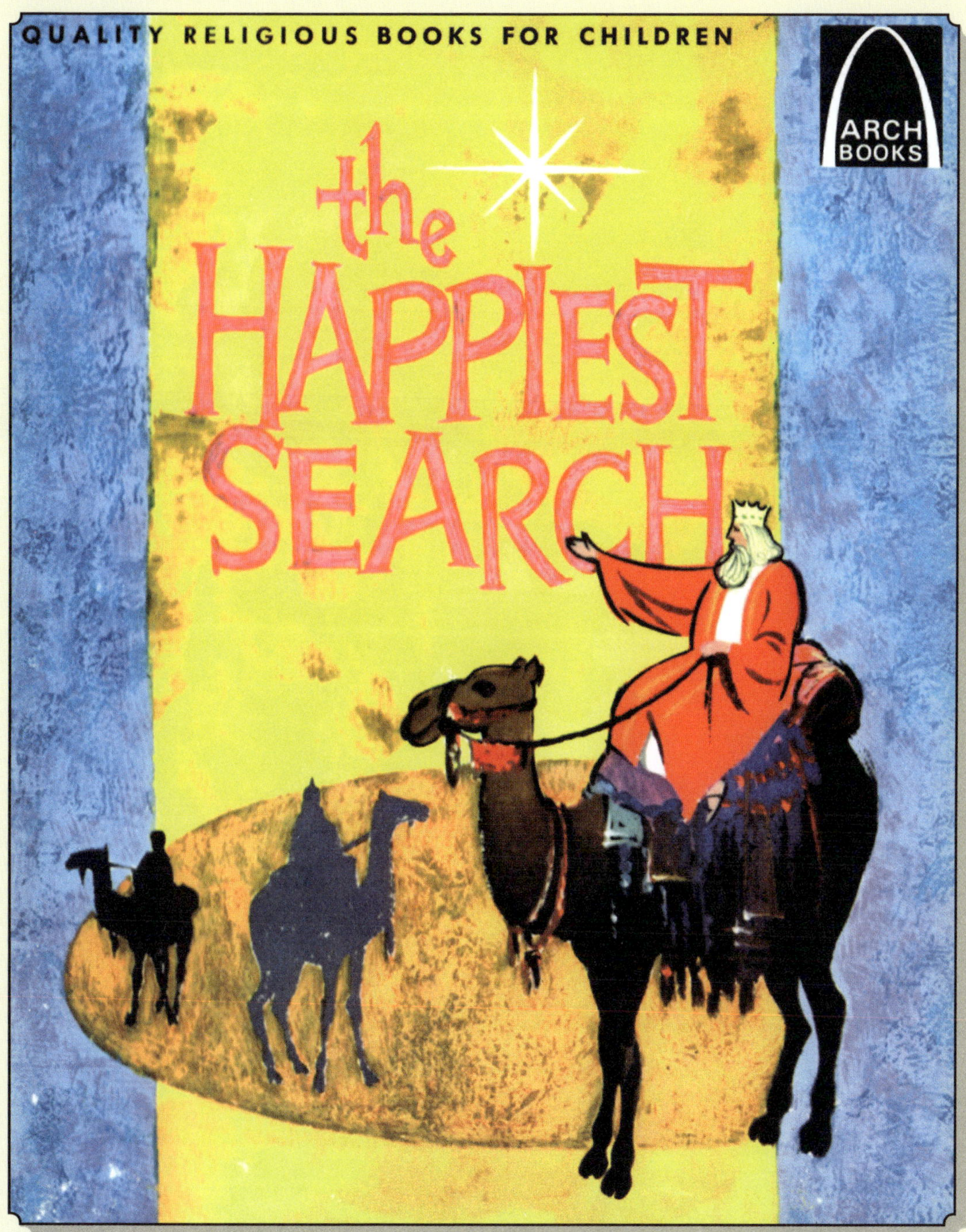
QUALITY RELIGIOUS BOOKS FOR CHILDREN
ARCH BOOKS
the
HAPPIEST
SEARCH

the HAPPIEST SEARCH

MATTHEW 2:1-11 AND LUKE 2:8-20 FOR CHILDREN

Written by Yvonne McCall

Illustrated by Sacred Design Associates

Concordia Publishing House

ARCH Books
COPYRIGHT © 1970 BY CONCORDIA PUBLISHING HOUSE,
ST. LOUIS, MISSOURI
CONCORDIA PUBLISHING HOUSE LTD., LONDON, E. C. 1
MANUFACTURED IN THE UNITED STATES OF AMERICA
ALL RIGHTS RESERVED
ISBN 0-570-06061-3

The gold was packed on the camel's back
with food for many a meal and snack
as they started out through the winter breeze
with fur cloaks bundled about their knees.

Loaded with precious gifts to bring,
they were off to search for a baby king.
"We'll cross the world from side to side,
and we'll find Him somewhere," the Wise Men cried.

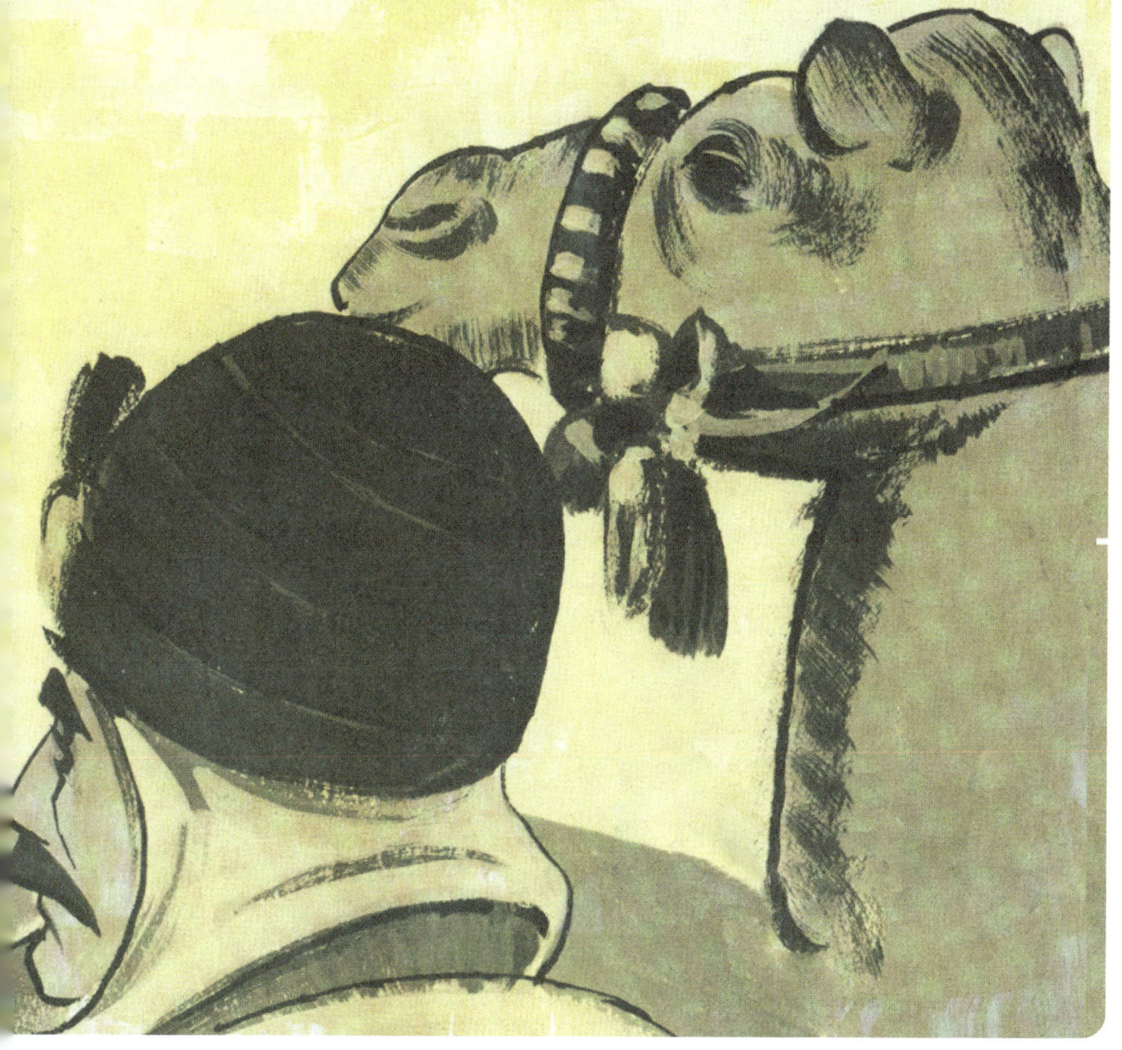

Before this, some hundreds of miles away,
near Bethlehem village, on Christmas Day
shepherds were guarding their flocks of sheep,
which were huddled together and fast asleep.

Suddenly there in the black of the night
an angel appeared in a blaze of light.
They froze in terror, then shook in dread.
But, "Don't be afraid," the angel said.
"I'll tell you my wonderful news right away.
Christ the Savior was born today,
a Lord for all people, each friend and stranger.
You'll find Him all bundled up in a manger."

More angels came to praise God, and then
they all disappeared into heaven again.
And the shepherds scurried as fast as they could
to the innkeeper's barn and a trough made of wood.

There, all wrapped up, the Baby lay
in the cattle's feedbox on bed of hay.
The shepherds were thrilled by this wondrous thing
and praised God for sending a Savior and King.

They spread their story, but none of them knew
that the Wise Men would come to worship Him too.
These traveled along through winter's rains
and summer's heat on desert plains.

To Jerusalem city they jolted and bounced.
"We've come on a trip from the East," they announce,
"for we saw there a star that proclaimed the news
that a baby was born King of the Jews."

They asked many people, in fact quite a few,
"Where is the Baby?" But nobody knew.

When Herod, the ruler, heard of their hunt,
he thought, "*I'm* the king. What more do they want?
I won't have another! I'll kill Him indeed."
And he sent for his scribes with the greatest of speed.

They gathered at once as the king had commanded.
"Now where was this Christ to be born?" he demanded.
They answered, "In Bethlehem village, we know,
for so it was forecast long, long ago."

King Herod then sent for the Wise Men three.
"The Child's in Bethlehem village," said he.
"Don't stop till you find Him. Search far and wide,
for I want to worship Him too," he lied.

So they started again on their trip with a sigh,
Then one of them shouted, "Look there! In the sky!"
As brilliant as ten thousand candles, at least,
was the wonderful star they had seen in the East.

It led them now by the light it was giving,
straight to the place where Jesus was living.
He was there in the house with Mary, His mother,
and they gave Him their treasures, first one, then another.

"We found Him at last," they joyfully cried
and knelt to worship at the little Boy's side.
For this was the Savior, the King, and His birth
was bringing God's peace to people on earth;
yes, this was God's reason for sending His Son,
and the wonderful story had only begun.

DEAR PARENTS:

The Wise Men, the shepherds, and King Herod searched for the baby King for different reasons and with different results.

The Wise Men and the shepherds searched with faith in God's Word. By a bright new star and the Scripture God guided the Wise Men to the newborn King of the Jews. To the shepherds God sent an angel to declare the good news that the long-promised Messiah had been born.

The Wise Men and the shepherds found their baby King and worshiped Him. The Wise Men were the first Gentiles and the shepherds were the first Jews to find the Savior. They worshiped the Babe, God's Son, with hearts aglow with joy and praise. The Wise Men gave their precious treasures to the baby King, who was God's precious gift of love to them. The shepherds gave to the infant Jesus their lips, with which they told the glad message of His lowly but royal birth. For He was God's message of the forgiveness of sins to them.

But Herod in his unbelief planned to find and kill the infant King. Herod feared the loss of his wealth and power to the baby King, whose only thrones were a manger and a cross and whose royal robes were swaddling clothes and a seamless garment. Herod never found the Savior and in death lost his wealth, his power, and his soul.

Will you help your children to seek more than merely the excitement of the birth of a child and presents under the Christmas tree? Will you rather help them in faith and joy to find in the baby King God's great gift of love, Jesus, who rescues them from their sin?

THE EDITOR

QUALITY RELIGIOUS BOOKS FOR CHILDREN

ARCH BOOKS

THE SECRET OF THE STAR

THE STORY OF THE WISE MEN

THE SECRET OF THE STAR

MATTHEW 2:1-12 FOR CHILDREN

Written by Dave Hill
Illustrated by Jim Roberts

Concordia Publishing House

ONCE, in a far-off Eastern land,
on a night so long ago,
a wise old man named Melchior
was pacing to and fro.

Now Melchior was a Magi priest,
who knew each star by sight.
"At least I DID," he told himself,
"until this star tonight
burst in the skies to dazzle my eyes,
and make me wonder why
one strange new star outshines by far
all others in the sky."

But he didn't know, and so … "Oh, ho!
Yes! That's the thing to do!
I'll send for Caspar and Balthasar!"
Perhaps … perhaps they knew.
He clapped his hands and gave commands,
sending for them to come.
"With three wise men … perhaps … why not?
Aren't three heads wiser than one?"

From the frost-painted North,
where the winter winds danced,
golden-haired Caspar came riding.

From the sun-blistered South,
where the summer breeze pranced,
came black, bearded Balthasar striding.

"You see that star?" said Melchior,
"Now — why is it so bright?"
"Perhaps it means," young Caspar said,
"that somewhere on this night
some great, great thing has come to pass."

"Of course!"

"That's it!"

"You're right!"

"Yes, yes, of course," they said as one,
"but now — just what great thing?"
"A battle?" "A war?" "A fire?" "A flood?"

"A poet?"

"A prince?"

"A king?"

"A KING! A KING!" they shouted in glee,
"A king is born tonight.
That's why this star shines from afar,
filling the earth with light!"
"I think...I read..." said Balthasar,
"in some old musty book...
About a star...to beckon from far..."
"To work!"
"To work!"
"Let's LOOK!"

They read, and read, and read some more,
until old Melchior spied
an ancient holy Jewish scroll:
"That's it! That's it!" he cried.

"See? — Read! It says a Star will come
from Jacob — which means the Jews.
Their King will rule the world in peace!
This star brought us the news!"

"Quick! Get a map! We'll have to go,
and gifts, too, we must bring.
God sent this star — we'll follow it
and worship this great King!"

"Load up the camels!"
old Melchior cried.
"This trip will take us far!"
The camels were packed,
and they set out,
led on by one bright star.

For days and days, and weeks and weeks,
through heat and wind and sand,
the star led on until at last
they reached the Holy Land.

"Jerusalem!" cried Melchior.
"We're there, beyond a doubt!
The star — it moves no more!"
"So now let's find the newborn King.
Let's go and search Him out.
We'll ask from door to door!"

"A King?"
"A Star?"
"No, I've not heard."
"A King's been born, you say?"

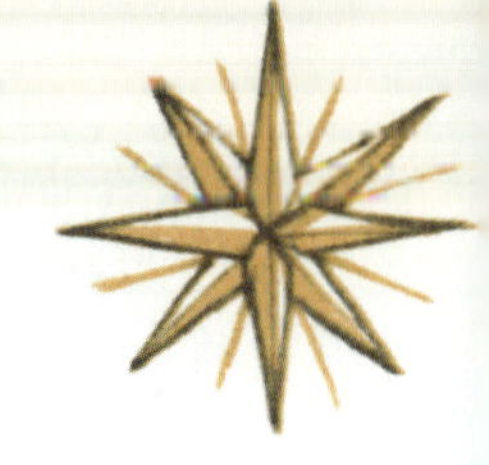

"A Prince?"
"Of Peace?"
"Don't be absurd!"
"You're mad — please go away!"

I'LL SHOW THEM

But old king Herod on his throne
soon heard of everything.
He sent his guards to bring them in —

WHO'S THE KING!

For in his heart the mighty king
was full of hate and fear.
"Another King? This can't be true!
I'll have no rivals here!"

H

"I hear you've come to see the king.
Well, look — for here I stand!"

But Melchior just shook his head,
"But, don't you understand?
We seek a Prince of Peace, and Love,
a Savior of the land!"

They left the king and searched
some more,
till Bethlehem they found.
"He's here! He's here!"
old Melchior cried.
"The star shines all around!"

They found the house
where Jesus was,
and knew at once that He
was God's own Prince of Peace —
the One they'd come so far to see!

They gave their gifts of frankincense
and myrrh and gold, and then
knelt down in awe to praise the Lord
for His great Gift to men.

"God sent the star," said Melchior,
"to lead us to the Lord.
We'll take the good news back with us!
We'll spread the joyous word!"

Then silently, with singing hearts
and wondrous news to bear,
they journeyed to their own home lands
to tell the people there
about the Prince of Peace God sent
to save men everywhere!

Dear Parents:

The story of the "wisemen," or the "magi," the learned astrologers from the East who were led by a star to the Christ Child, is a story of the Light given to the Gentiles (nations) in Christ the Messiah. The appearing of Christ to the world is what we celebrated on Epiphany, the "Twelfth Day of Christmas."

For about 2,000 years the descendants of Abraham formed a people apart from the rest of the nations. It was in their history that God made His ways and will known, preparing for Himself a people that would bring His revelation to the ends of the earth when the time was ripe. The promise was that at the coming of the Messiah the "nations" should flock to the Light come to Israel (Is. 60:1-6). Those who did not know God's glory should then receive a "sign" and come and see it (Is. 66:18-21). This was now beginning to be fulfilled with the coming of the wisemen, whom ancient Christian tradition sees as three men named Caspar, Balthasar, and Melchior, symbolically representing all the different peoples of the earth.

Will you help your child see the excitement involved in the sign given to these heathen magi inviting them to see and welcome the Christ Child, the Prince of Peace, the Savior and King of all the earth? You may want to act out their journey and celebrate their happy arrival and thus discover a meaningful way to close the Christmas season.

THE EDITOR

QUALITY RELIGIOUS BOOKS FOR CHILDREN
ARCH BOOKS
CLEM, THE CLUMSY CAMEL

CLEM, THE CLUMSY CAMEL

Matthew 2:1-12 FOR CHILDREN

Written by Virginia Mueller

Illustrated by Betty Wind

A camel by the name of Clem
Was left at home each day,
While other well-trained camels
Went to places far away.

"I'm clumsy when I kneel," sighed Clem,
"I'm clumsy when I rise,"
And two big tears of sadness
Rolled out of Clem's brown eyes.

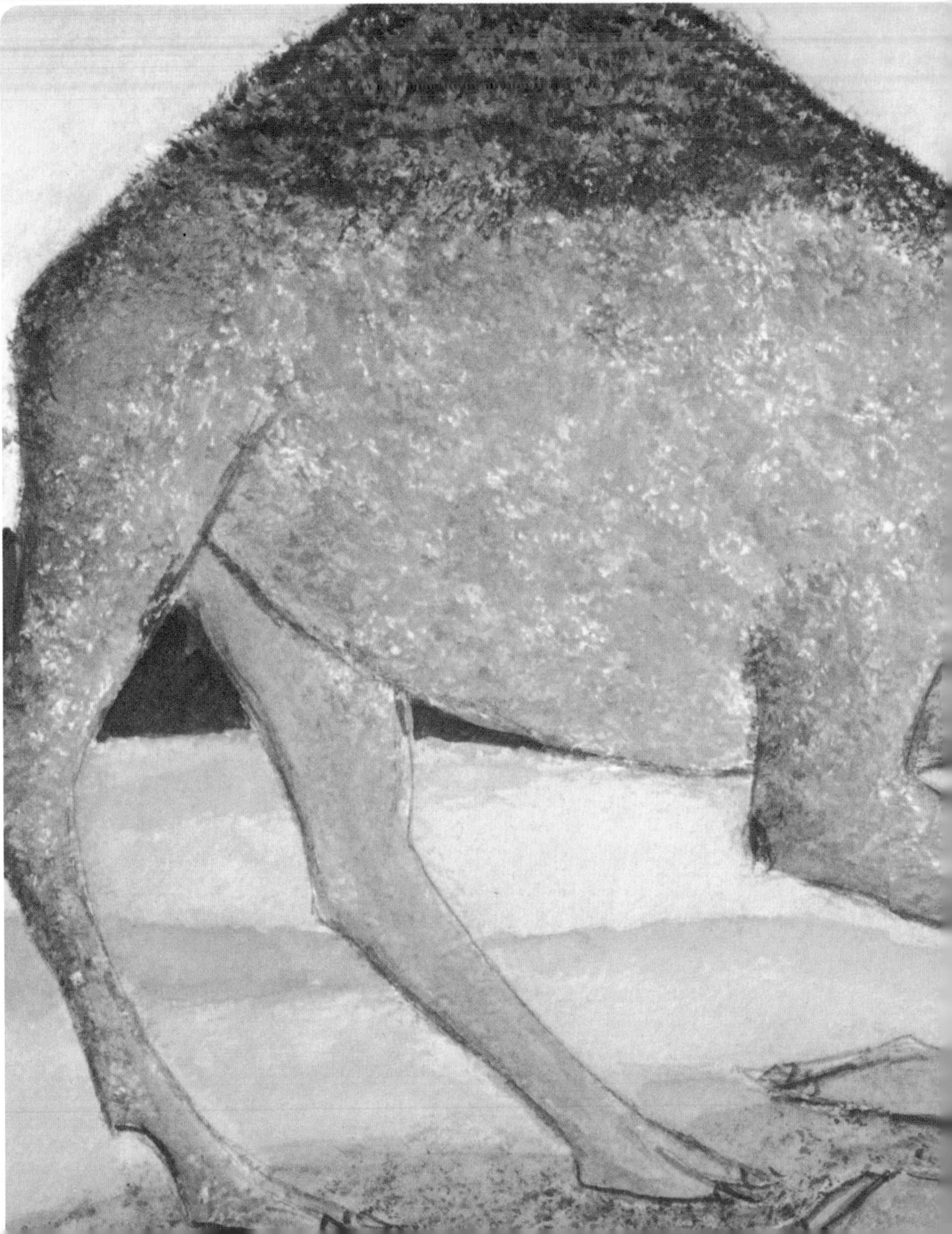

Each day he practiced kneeling
But tumbled to his nose;
And when he practiced rising,
He stubbed his four front toes.

"A camel who is clumsy,"
Said the trainer with a shrug,
"Will end up as an Arab's tent,
A blanket, or a rug.

"To be in camel caravans
Your lessons you must learn.
When you can kneel and rise with ease,
A silver bell you'll earn."

"I better keep on trying,"
Said Clem, "so I can be
A big 'ship of the desert'
And sail a sandy sea.

"I'll carry loads—a thousand pounds
Of rare and precious things.
Perfumes so fragrant, spices rare,
And jewels fit for kings.

"I'll cross the sandy desert
And stop at each oasis
To talk with other camels
About interesting places.

"The palace of King Herod —
Hanging gardens, towers tall,
Temples, seaports, pyramids —
I will see them all."

That night while Clem lay sleeping,
He opened one big eye
And saw a brightly shining star
Move across the sky.

Not far away, a Magi priest
Observed the bright star too.
Said Melchior, "That star is strange.
It must be something new."

So Melchior consulted
With Wise Man Balthasar,
Then sent for Wise Man Caspar
Who had also seen the star.

They checked through
    musty records.
They read an ancient book.

Said Melchior,
    "There's one more place,
Where I think that
    we should look."

They found a holy Jewish scroll,
And there the Wise Men spied
Some prophecy about a star,
"This is the clue!" they cried.

"This ancient Jewish scroll predicts
A new star will appear
To mark the birthplace of a King.
That time must now be here.

"Let's leave tonight. We'll follow it."
The Wise Men all agreed.
"But first we must buy camels.
Their help we'll surely need."

They bargained with the trainer
Who sold those three Wise Men
Two big, ill-tempered camels
And a clumsy one called Clem.

Clem proudly kneeled to get his load.
He wobbled just a little.
And when he rose to start the march,
He wiggled in the middle.

The loads were packed so off they went,
Led on by one bright star.
"We'll travel night and day," they said.
"This trip will take us far."

The big, ill-tempered camels
Complained and kicked and grumbled,
But Clem was cheerful all the way
And very seldom stumbled.

They rocked and rolled and humped and bumped
Through valley, rock, and sand,

Until high in the hills ahead
They saw the Holy Land.

The Wise Men went to Herod's court;
He ordered them to go
And seek the babe in Bethlehem,
Just where he did not know.

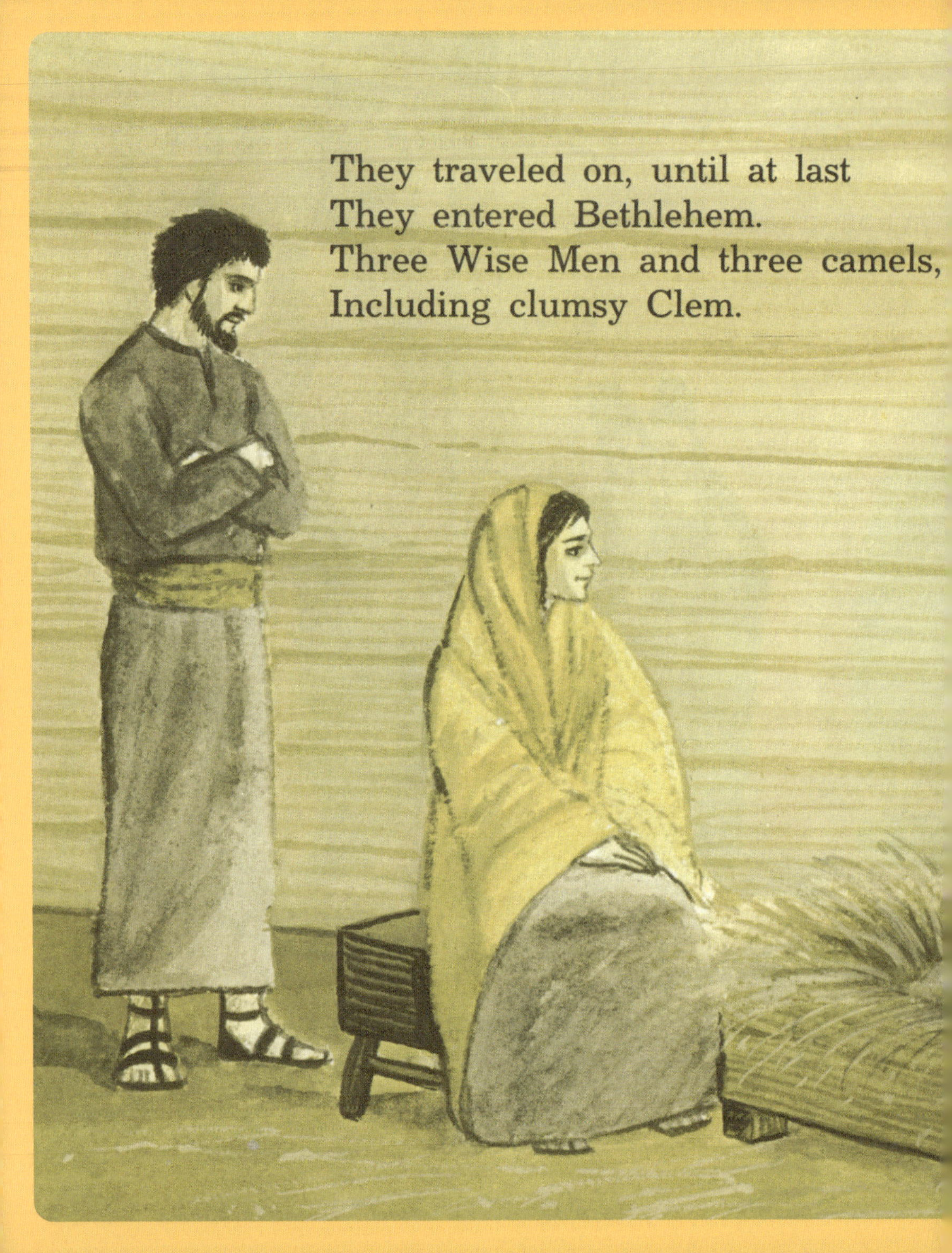

They traveled on, until at last
They entered Bethlehem.
Three Wise Men and three camels,
Including clumsy Clem.

Clem saw the Wise Men bring their gifts;
He saw them kneeling too.
Then Clem the clumsy camel
Knew just what he should do.

He followed their example,
And in that holy place
He knelt and rose—just perfectly—
With regal camel grace.

Dear Parents:

Being a clumsy camel must have been a great hardship for Clem. After all, no one would enjoy living under the threat of someday becoming a blanket or a rug in an Arab's tent! What caused Clem to shed his clumsiness is the real message of this book, the message that can be transferred to our own lives.

All of us are clumsy in one way; we call that clumsiness "sin." God recognized our clumsiness and devised a divine plan to make us grace-full. That plan was fulfilled on a long-ago Christmas night. Because of the gift God sent that night, we can get up again when our clumsiness causes us to fall. We can have as many fresh starts as we need. We can walk forever in the light of God's love and filled with His grace.

Ask your child if he is ever sad because he has failed in some way. Maybe he did something wrong on purpose, or maybe it was an accident. Why did God send His Son to us on the first Christmas? How can remembering that make us feel better when we fail?

Assure him that God never stops loving us, even when we do fail. He forgives us and wants us to stop being sad and try again. He even helps us to do better. And, most important, He has sent us His Son, Jesus, to save us from our clumsy sins.

The Editor

Bible Beginnings

592287 Falling into Sin
592206 A Man Named Noah
591511 Noah's 2-by-2 Adventure
591560 The Story of Creation
592239 Where Did the World Come From?

The Old Testament

591502 Abraham's Big Test
592244 Abraham, Sarah, and Isaac
592283 Cain and Abel
592229 Daniel and the Lions
591593 David and His Friend Jonathan
592220 Deborah Saves the Day
591543 Elijah Helps the Widow
592251 Ezekiel and the Dry Bones
591567 The Fiery Furnace
591587 God Provides Victory
            through Gideon
592279 God Saves Jerusalem
591523 God's Fire for Elijah
591542 Good News for Naaman
592223 How Enemies Became Friends
592247 Isaac Blesses Jacob and Esau
591538 Jacob's Dream
591539 Jericho's Tumbling Walls
592246 Jonah, the Runaway Prophet
591514 Jonah and the Very Big Fish
592233 Joseph, Jacob's Favorite Son
592290 Joshua and the Battle of Jericho
592216 King Josiah and God's Book
591583 The Lord Calls Samuel
592219 Moses and the Bronze Snake
591607 Moses and the Long Walk
592266 The Mystery of the Moving Hand
591535 A Mother Who Prayed
592249 One Boy, One Stone, One God
592253 Queen Esther Visits the King
592211 Ruth and Naomi
592276 Samson
591586 The Ten Commandments
591608 The Ten Plagues
592263 The Tower of Babel
591550 Tiny Baby Moses
591530 Tried and True Job
592260 The 23rd Psalm

The New Testament

591580 The Coming of the Holy Spirit
592259 The Great Commission
591532 Jailhouse Rock
591520 Jesus and the Family Trip
592277 Jesus and the Rich Young Man
592215 Jesus Shows His Glory
591521 Mary and Martha's Dinner Guest
592269 Nicodemus and Jesus
592227 Paul's Great Basket Caper

592267 The Pentecost Story
592289 Peter Surprises Rhoda
591578 Philip and the Ethiopian
591601 Saul's Conversion
591574 Timothy Joins Paul
592222 Twelve Ordinary Men
592282 Where Is Jesus?
591599 Zacchaeus

Arch® Book Companions

592299 Arch Books Treasury: Christmas
            Collection
592295 Arch Books Treasury: Life of Jesus
592281 Arch Books Treasury: Vintage
            Collection 1964–1965
592285 Arch Books Treasury: Vintage
            Collection 1966–1967
592232 The Fruit of the Spirit
591609 God, I've Gotta Talk to You
591575 The Lord's Prayer
591562 My Happy Birthday Book
592271 Best-Loved Christmas Stories
592272 Best-Loved Parables of Jesus
592273 Best-Loved Miracles of Jesus
592274 Best-Loved Easter Stories

Christmas Arch® Books

591579 Baby Jesus Is Born
591544 Baby Jesus Visits the Temple
591553 Born on Christmas Morn
592292 The Baby King
592261 The Christmas Angels
592286 The Christmas Connection
592225 The Christmas Promise
591499 Mary's Christmas Story
591584 My Merry Christmas Arch® Book
592278 O Bethlehem
592252 Oh, Holy Night!
591537 On a Silent Night
592243 Once Upon a Clear Dark Night
592234 The Shepherds Shook in Their Shoes
592268 The Songs of Christmas
591594 Star of Wonder
592209 When Jesus Was Born

Easter Arch® Books

592205 The Centurion at the Cross
591516 The Day Jesus Died
592213 The Easter Gift
592221 The Easter Stranger
592275 The Easter Surprise
591602 The Easter Victory
592265 From Adam to Easter
591582 Good Friday
592291 Jesus Christ Is Risen Today!
591585 Jesus Enters Jerusalem
591561 Jesus Returns to Heaven
592248 John's Easter Story

591592 Mary Magdalene's Easter Story
591564 My Happy Easter Arch® Book
592258 The Gardens of Easter
592284 The Night Peter Cried
592231 The Resurrection
591517 The Story of the Empty Tomb
591504 Thomas, the Doubting Disciple
591501 The Very First Lord's Supper
591541 The Week That Led to Easter

Parables and Lessons of Jesus

592257 Jesus and the Canaanite Woman
591589 Jesus and the Woman at the Well
591500 Jesus Blesses the Children
591595 Jesus, My Good Shepherd
592245 Jesus Teaches Us Not to Worry
592294 Jesus Visits Mary and Martha
591540 Jesus Washes Peter's Feet
592264 The Lesson of the Tree and Its Fruit
591606 The Lost Coin
592235 The Parable of the Ten Bridesmaids
592218 The Parable of the Lost Sheep
592224 The Parable of the Prodigal Son
592262 The Parable of the Seeds
592210 The Parable of the Talents
592254 The Parable of the Woman
            and the Judge
592250 The Parable of the Workers
            in the Vineyard
591512 The Seeds That Grew and Grew
591503 The Story of Jesus' Baptism
            and Temptation
591596 The Story of the Good Samaritan
592214 The Widow's Offering
592208 The Wise and Foolish Builders

Miracles Jesus Performed

591531 Down through the Roof
591568 Get Up, Lazarus!
591604 The Great Catch of Fish
592288 Hungry Mouths, Hungry Hearts
592293 Jesus' Beach Breakfast
591581 Jesus Calms the Storm
591598 Jesus' First Miracle
592230 Jesus Heals Blind Bartimaeus
592255 Jesus Heals the Man at the Pool
592236 Jesus Heals the Centurion's Servant
592226 Jesus Wakes the Little Girl
591597 Jesus Walks on the Water
592212 The Thankful Leper
592280 The Wedding at Cana
591510 What's for Lunch?

Please visit **cph.org/archbooks** to browse our complete list of available titles.